THE

3

INGREDIENT

COOKBOOK

VOLUME 1

by
Ruthie Wornall

Three Ingredient Cookbook

VOLUME I

*A Collection of Favorite Recipes
Compiled By*

Ruthie Wornall

A Word of Thanks. . .

"A recipe not shared with others
will soon be forgotten."

I wish to express my sincere appreciation and thanks to all those individuals who donated recipes or in any other way contributed to the publication of this cookbook.

Additional copies of this cookbook can be purchased by sending **$6.95** per copy, plus **$2.00** postage to:

Ruthie Wornall
9800 W. 104th Street
Overland Park, Kansas 66212
(913) 888-1530

ISBN 0-9624467-0-X

Printed by:

Blue & Grey Book Shoppe
107 W. Lexington, Independence, MO 64050
1-816-252-9909
http://blueandgrey.com

FIRST PRINTING
December 1988

TWENTY-NINTH PRINTING
February 1999

36,448 books now in print!

Three Ingredient Cookbook
Volume I
by
Ruthie Wornall

The **Three Ingredient Cookbook** is written for busy people who have limited time to devote to meal preparation, as well as for new brides or for children who are learning to cook. This book makes it easy to cook.

Not only are the recipes simple, fast, easy, and tasty, they are also economical since each requires only three ingredients. The book incorporates short-cuts into many of the recipes which saves time, but does not compromise taste.

This book is the first of a series of Three Ingredient Cookbooks. Each cookbook contains 175 recipes, and entire dinners can be prepared from each book as there are recipes in all categories ranging from appetizers, beverages, soups, salads, and vegetables to main dishes, breads, and desserts.

This is a cookbook you will reach for again and again.

FAVORITE RECIPES
FROM MY COOKBOOK

Recipe Name	Page Number

Appetizers
Beverages

Appetizer & Beverage Hints

• Try 1/2 cup plain yogurt, 2 packages low-cal sweetener, and 2 table-spoons of vanilla mixed together for a cereal topping, a decorative dessert topping or an appetite appeaser. It is also a good source of calcium.

• For a quick, low calorie dip, blend one 12-ounce carton of cottage cheese, 2 tablespoons of lemon juice, and a desired amount of Good Season's Italian dry dressing. Mix in blender until smooth and refrigerate until ready to use.

• Use pretzel sticks instead of toothpicks when serving cubes of cheese. Stick one pretzel into your favorite cheese cube for added flavor and ease of handling.

• For a crispy, novel sandwich, prepare sandwich with a filling that's not too moist. Lightly butter the outside of both sides of the sandwich and bake in your waffle iron.

• Nuts will come out of the shell in halves if soaked overnight in salt water before cracking. After cracking black walnuts, let stand overnight and they can be removed from the shell more easily.

• Keep unpopped popcorn in the freezer to help eliminate unpopped kernels.

• Sprinkle popcorn lightly with warm water and let stand a few hours before popping. The added moisture makes it pop better.

• Slip plastic bags onto your hands when shaping popcorn balls. They won't stick to your hands or burn them.

• Rub a little butter over cheese that isn't to be used right away and it won't harden.

• Spread a cored apple ring with cream cheese or peanut butter. Top with a second cored apple ring.

• Dip ends of carrot, celery or cucumber sticks into softened cream cheese. Sprinkle with minced parsley.

• Combine 3 ounces cream cheese, softened, and 2 1/2 ounces deviled ham. Blend well. Use to stuff bite-sized pieces of celery.

• Tomato tempter: Combine 3/4 cup cold milk, 1/2 cup tomato-vegetable cocktail juice, 1/2 teaspoon Worcestershire sauce, and salt to taste. Blend well. Makes 1 serving.

• Flavored milk drink: Shake together 1/2 cup cold milk and 1/2 cup orange, prune or apple juice. Pour into chilled glass. Makes 1 serving. Flavored milk also can be made with 1/2 cup unsweetened pineapple or grape juice and 1/2 cup cold milk.

• For easy reference, tape the measurements and directions to the lids of containers of coffee, tea or rice.

• For hot beverages, use freshly drawn cold water and boil as little as possible.

• Make your own Swiss Mocha drink by using 1 teaspoon instant coffee and 1 teaspoon hot cocoa mix. It's delicious.

APPETIZERS, BEVERAGES

SAUSAGE BALLS

2 c. Bisquick mix
1 lb. hot sausage (R.B. Rice)

1 c. shredded Cheddar cheese

Mix the 3 ingredients together with your hands. Shape into balls. Place on jelly roll pan and bake at 350°F. for 20 minutes. These freeze well. Makes about 3 dozen small balls.

TUNA BALL

8 oz. cream cheese, softened
½ pkg. Lipton's dry onion soup
 mix

1 (6¼ oz.) can white albacore
 tuna, drained (or any tuna
 you prefer)

Combine ingredients; mix well. Shape into a ball. Chill 4 to 6 hours. Serve with crackers, chips, or raw vegetables. Serves 8.

EASY CHEESE BALL

2 small jars Old English sharp
 cheese
Nuts, finely chopped

2 (3 oz.) pkg. cream cheese,
 softened

Combine cheese and cream cheese. Mix well, then shape into a ball. Chill 4 to 6 hours.
Roll cheese ball in chopped nuts. Wrap in Saran Wrap until time to serve. Serves 8.

ORANGE FRUIT DIP

1 (8 oz.) pkg. Philadelphia cream
 cheese, softened
¼ c. chopped nuts

1 or 2 Tbsp. Tang orange drink
 mix

Combine, mix well, and chill.
Serve in small bowl in the middle of a platter surrounded by sliced apples.
Serving idea: Cut a top slice off of an apple or an orange. Then scoop the pulp from the fruit. (Sprinkle lemon juice over the apple cup, if apple is used.) Fill the fruit cup with the dip. Makes about 1 cup.

CHEESE SQUARES

2 lb. Velveeta cheese
3 to 5 tsp. Tabasco hot sauce

1 c. finely chopped nuts

Melt cheese in top of double boiler over hot water. Stir in nuts and hot sauce. Mix well. Pour into a greased 9x13 inch pan. Chill until firm. Cut into squares. Serve with crackers. Serves 12 to 16.

HAM PINWHEELS

9 thin slices of cooked ham
9 pickle sticks

1 small jar olive-pimento spread

Spread thin slices of cooked ham with olive-pimento spread (or cream cheese). Lay a pickle stick on it, then roll up. Slice or serve as pinwheels. (Secure with wooden picks.) Makes about 3 dozen.

STUFFED CHERRY TOMATOES

12 cherry tomatoes
½ chopped onion

1 (8 oz.) pkg. Philadelphia cream cheese, softened

Combine cream cheese and onion. Mix well. Cut tomatoes in halves. Drain on paper towels. Scoop out pulp and mix into cream cheese. Stuff tomatoes. Cover and chill. Makes 24.

ARTICHOKE DIP

1 can drained artichoke hearts, chopped

1 c. Parmesan cheese
1 c. mayonnaise

Combine the 3 ingredients, mix well and pour into a greased baking dish. Bake 20 to 30 minutes at 350°F.
Serve with fresh vegetables, chips or crackers. Serves 8 to 12.

FRUIT DIP

1 (8 oz.) pkg. cream cheese, softened

Confectioners sugar (to taste)
½ tsp. vanilla

Combine, mix, and chill. Serve with fresh fruits (strawberries, apples, etc.). Makes 1 cup.

EGGPLANT PORCUPINE

1 large eggplant
Cheddar cheese, cubed

Olives

Cut slice from an eggplant bottom so it will stand upright. Place in center of a dish.

Thread cheese cube, olive and a second cheese cube on wooden picks. Insert in eggplant. Completely cover until the eggplant looks like a porcupine full of quills.

SHRIMP SURPRISE

¼ c. shrimp cocktail sauce (or more)
8 oz. Philadelphia cream cheese

1 to 2 cans tiny shrimp, cooked, drained, and chilled

Place bar of cream cheese in center of a serving plate. Pour cocktail sauce over cheese. Sprinkle cooled shrimp over sauce. Surround with crackers. Serves 8 to 12.

BLACK OLIVE SPREAD

1 small can chopped black olives
1 (8 oz.) pkg. shredded Cheddar cheese

1 (3 oz.) pkg. Philadelphia cream cheese

Combine olives and the 2 cheeses. (Optional: Mix in 3 chopped green onions.)

Spread on slices of party rye or pumpernickel bread. Serve cold, or broil and serve hot. Serves 6 to 8.

HOT CHEESE DIP

1 lb. Velveeta cheese
1 (10 oz.) can Ro-Tel tomatoes, drained

1 to 2 chopped green onions or chives

Melt Velveeta cheese in top of double boiler. Stir in 1 can drained Ro-Tel tomatoes. Sprinkle chopped green onions or chives over top.

Serve with Fritos or tortilla chips. Serves 8 to 12.

MARY SUTTON'S SALAMI-OLIVE WRAPS

8 salami slices
1 or 2 (3 oz.) pkg. cream cheese, softened

1 small jar green olives (stuffed with pimento)

Cut salami into 2 to 3 inch strips. Spread each strip with softened Philadelphia cream cheese. Place one olive in center of salami strip. Roll up and hold with wooden pick. Makes about 24.

BACON-CHEESE FINGERS

8 rye bread slices   8 slices bacon (2 to 3 inch pieces)
8 Cheddar cheese slices

Cut rye bread in 2 to 3 inch rectangles, then toast in oven. Fry bacon (cut in 2 to 3 inch pieces) until crisp. Drain on paper towels. Cut cheese into 2 to 3 inch strips.

To assemble, lay crisp bacon on top of toast. Top with cheese. Broil until cheese melts. Makes 24.

RED CABBAGE BASKET OF DIP

Red cabbage   12 oz. sour cream
Lipton's dry onion soup mix

Combine dry onion soup mix with sour cream. Mix the dip well.

Cut top off of a washed red cabbage. Hollow out to form a basket or cup. Fill with onion dip.

Place in center of platter and surround it with fresh veggies: Carrot sticks, celery, olives, zucchini sticks, etc. Or serve with chips or Fritos, if preferred. Serves 12.

CHIPPED BEEF BALLS

1 (4 oz.) pkg. chipped beef   1 to 2 Tbsp. chopped onion
2 (3 oz.) pkg. cream cheese

Spread a thin layer of chipped beef in a shallow pan; place in a 350°F. oven until dry and crisp, about 15 minutes. Cool. Crumble dried beef. Set aside.

Combine cream cheese and onion. Shape into small balls. Roll in crumbled dried beef until beef coats the balls. Serve on wooden picks. Makes 1½ to 2 dozen.

BAKED LACY CHEESE

2 (8 oz.) bars Monterey Jack   Crackers
   cheese   Pam cooking spray

Thinly slice or cube Monterey Jack cheese. Spray a jelly roll pan with Pam. Place small cubes of cheese on pan 2 inches apart. Bake at 400°F. for 2 to 3 minutes until melted and lacy.

Serve with crackers (or with seedless grapes).

HOT APPLE CIDER

2 qt. apple cider   ½ c. cinnamon red hot candies
1 apple, sliced

Pour 2 quarts apple cider into a large pan. Stir in ½ cup red hot candies. Simmer until candy has dissolved.
Serve hot in mugs. Garnish with ½ apple slice. Makes 2 quarts.

CRANBERRY PUNCH

2 qt. chilled cranberry juice   2 small cans frozen lemonade
2 qt. chilled ginger ale   concentrate

Combine, mix, and pour into punch bowl. Add 2 cans water, if needed. Makes about 1 gallon.

HAWAIIAN PUNCH

1 (46 oz.) can Hawaiian punch,   1 (12 oz.) can frozen lemonade
   chilled   concentrate
1 (2 liter) bottle chilled ginger ale

Combine the ingredients in a punch bowl. Mix in 4 cups cold water. Makes 20 to 24 cups of punch.

STRAWBERRY PUNCH

2 (6 oz.) cans frozen pink   1 (2 liter) bottle of 7-Up or ginger
   lemonade   ale, chilled
2 small boxes strawberries

Thaw berries until slushy (or mix in blender). Pour lemonade into punch bowl and stir in berries. Add 7-Up or ginger ale and stir until well blended. (If this punch is too tart, you might wish to add sugar.) Serves 20 to 25.

ANNA MARIE'S LOW-CAL PUNCH

1 (2 liter) diet 7-Up, chilled   1 (46 oz.) can Dole pineapple
1 (12 oz.) can frozen Minute Maid   juice, chilled
   lemonade

Combine in punch bowl and mix well. (Recipe can be doubled.) Add an ice ring to the punch bowl, if you wish. Makes about 25 (4 ounce) cups.

PINEAPPLE PUNCH

4 qt. ginger ale, chilled
2 qt. pineapple sherbet

1 small can pineapple tidbits, chilled

Combine ginger ale, pineapple sherbet and ½ cup pineapple tidbits. Mix. Serve in punch bowl. Serves about 30.

LIME PUNCH

½ gal. lime sherbet
2 (2 liter) bottles 7-Up, chilled

1 (2 liter) bottle ginger ale, chilled

Combine, mix and serve in punch bowl. Makes about 40 (4 ounce) cups.

SUN TEA

8 regular-size tea bags
1 gal. cold water

Lemon slices

Put 8 regular-size tea bags in a gallon jar and fill with cold water. Set jar in sunshine for 3 to 4 hours.
Serve over ice with lemon slice (or sprig of mint). Serves 8 to 12.

HOLIDAY PUNCH

1 pkg. cherry Kool-Aid
2 qt. ginger ale, chilled

1 (46 oz.) can pineapple juice, chilled

Combine; mix well. Add more ginger ale if needed.
Serve in punch bowl. Serves 20 to 25.

CRANBERRY CREAM PUNCH

1 c. cranberry juice cocktail
1 large scoop vanilla ice cream

8 oz. plain yogurt

For 2 to 3 servings, combine cranberry juice, yogurt and ice cream in a blender. Serves 2.

STRAWBERRY PUNCH

3 cans (46 oz.) pineapple juice, chilled

10 (12 oz.) cans strawberry pop
1 (2 liter) bottle 7-Up

Pour 2 cans (46 ounce) pineapple juice into a punch bowl. Mix in 10 (12 ounce) cans of strawberry pop. Stir in a 2 liter bottle of 7-Up.

A few hours before preparing the punch, freeze 1 (46 ounce) can of pineapple juice in 8 empty butter tubs.

When ready to serve, add 1 to 2 tubs of frozen juice to the punch to keep it cold. Continue adding tubs as needed. Serves 50 to 60.

ROSEBILLIE'S COCOA MIX

3 c. dry powdered milk   ⅓ c. cocoa
1 c. sugar

Mix well.

Use 6 level tablespoons to each cup of hot water to make a cup of hot chocolate.

Optional: Top each cup with a marshmallow.

Soups
Salads
Vegetables

Hints for Salads

- When buying grapefruit, judge it by its weight. The heavier ones are juicier.
- Add 1/4 teaspoon soda to cranberries while cooking and they will not require as much sugar.
- Frosted Grapes: Beat 2 egg whites and 2 tablespoons water slightly. Dip small clusters of grapes into the mixture. Sprinkle with granulated sugar. Dry on waxed paper.
- Lemons that are heated before squeezing will give almost twice the quantity of juice.
- Lemon juice on cut bananas will keep them from darkening.
- Grease the salad mold with salad dressing, mayonnaise or salad oil and it will help the salad slip out easily.
- Save sweet pickle juice. Store it in the refrigerator and use small amounts to thin dressings for salads.
- Soak hard-cooked eggs in beet pickle juice for an interesting taste and colorful garnish.
- To make a hard-cooked egg flower: Cut white from the small end of the egg about 3/4 of the way down, petal fashion, being careful not to cut yolk. When spread apart, these white petals should show yolk as a round ball, daisy fashion. Slice green pepper for leaves. Nice for potato salad.
- Marshmallows will cut easily if the blades of the scissors are buttered.
- Try putting marshmallows in the refrigerator and they won't stick to the scissors.
- Perk up soggy lettuce by adding lemon juice to a bowl of cold water and soaking it for an hour in the refrigerator.
- The darker, outer leaves of lettuce are higher in calcium, iron and Vitamin A.
- Do not add salt to a lettuce salad until just before serving; salt makes the lettuce wilt and become tough.
- Toss salads well so you can use less dressing which is healthier.
- Prepare ingredients such as greens, chopped onions, celery, carrots and radishes ahead of time. Store in separate airtight containers for quick use in a tossed salad.
- When you will be doing extra cooking, keep shredded cheese, bread crumbs, and chopped onion on hand for use in salads, casseroles and vegetables.
- Before grating cheese, brush vegetable oil on the grater and it will clean easier.
- Remove the tops of carrots before storing. Tops absorb moisture and nutrients from the carrots.
- It is easy to remove the white membrane from oranges - for fancy desserts or salads - by soaking them in boiling water for 5 minutes before you peel them.
- Lemon Jello, dissolved in 2 cups of hot apricot nectar with 1 teaspoon of grated lemon added for zip, makes a perfect base for jelled fruit salad.

SOUPS, SALADS, VEGETABLES

EASY STEAK SOUP

2 lb. ground round steak   1 (20 oz.) pkg. frozen vegetables
46 oz. can V-8 juice

    Brown ground round steak and drain. Combine V-8 juice and frozen vegetables with meat and bring to boil. Simmer 20 minutes. Serves 6 to 8.
    Optional: Add chopped onion.

NO-PEEK STEW

2 lb. beef stew meat, cubed, fat   1 (10 oz.) can mushroom soup
  trimmed   1 pkg. onion soup mix

    Combine and mix well. Stir in 1 cup water. Cover; bake for 2½ to 3 hours at 300° to 325°. Do not peek! Optional: Serve over rice or noodles. Serves 6.

TOMATO-BACON SOUP

1 (10 oz.) can Campbell's tomato   ½ lb. bacon, fried, drained and
  soup   crumbled
1 (16 oz.) can stewed tomatoes
  (with celery and peppers)

    Combine soup and stewed tomatoes. Heat thoroughly. Sprinkle bacon over soup and serve hot. Serves 4.
    Good with grilled cheese sandwiches.

ONION SOUP

2 (10 oz.) cans onion soup   1 c. shredded Swiss or Cheddar
4 French bread slices   cheese

    Heat soups. Pour into 4 ovenproof soup bowls or mugs. Top each mug with one slice of French bread and enough cheese to cover the bread. Bake 10 minutes or until the cheese melts. Serves 4.

PINTO BEAN SOUP

2 pkg. dry pinto beans   Smoked ham hocks
Salt to taste

Wash beans. Cover with cold water and soak overnight.

Next day: Drain and re-cover beans with water. Bring to boil. Add smoked ham hock. Reduce heat and simmer slowly for 4 to 5 hours. Season with salt to taste. <u>Great with corn bread!</u> Serves 6.

POTATO SOUP

2 (10 oz.) cans potato soup   Bacon, fried, drained and
Shredded Cheddar cheese   crumbled

Heat potato soup thoroughly. (May mix 1 cup milk into soup, if desired.)

Fry bacon until crisp; drain and crumble.

Pour soup into soup bowls. Top with 1 or 2 tablespoons of Cheddar cheese and desired amount of bacon. Serves 4.

CREAMY CRANBERRY MOLD

2 (3 oz.) pkg. cherry Jell-O   1 (16 oz.) can jellied cranberry
1 c. sour cream   sauce

Dissolve Jell-O in 2 cups of boiling water. Stir in cranberry sauce. Mix until well blended. Add sour cream and beat in an electric mixer until creamy. Pour into a mold and chill until firm. Serves 6 to 8.

CINNAMON APPLE SALAD

⅔ c. cinnamon red hot candies   1 (3 oz.) pkg. cherry Jell-O
1½ c. Musselman's applesauce

Heat cinnamon red hots in ⅔ cup boiling water until candy melts. Pour over dry Jell-O and stir until well dissolved.

Chill until partially set. Stir in applesauce. Refrigerate until firm. Serves 4.

CHICKEN SALAD VERONIQUE

2 c. diced, cooked chicken breasts   Mayonnaise
1 c. seedless grapes

Combine chicken, grapes and mayonnaise. Mix well and chill.

Optional: Stir in ⅔ teaspoon curry powder (or slivered almonds). Serves 4.

STUFFED TOMATO SALAD

4 to 6 tomatoes   1 chopped onion
Cottage cheese

Cut each tomato ¾ of way down into 6 wedges, then separate wedges slightly. Turn upside down and drain on napkins. (Or cut off top of tomato and scoop out pulp, then drain.)

Combine cottage cheese and onion. Mix and fill tomato cavity.

For variation: Stuff tomatoes with tuna salad instead of cottage cheese. Serves 4 to 6.

CRANBERRY ORANGE RELISH

1 (15 oz.) can whole berry   ⅔ c. orange marmalade
    cranberries, drained   ⅓ c. black walnuts

Combine, mix, cover, and chill 2–3 hours before serving. Serves 4.

SPINACH-ORANGE SALAD

2 c. spinach, washed and torn   1 can mandarin oranges, drain
    into pieces   juice, but reserve
⅓ c. toasted slivered almonds

Toss together. Sprinkle with juice from mandarin oranges. Serves 4.

Optional: Sprinkle with poppy seeds.
Optional: Toss with vinegar and oil dressing.

TUNA ARTICHOKE SALAD

2 (6 oz.) cans albacore white tuna   Mayonnaise
    fish (or any tuna)
1 (16 oz.) can artichoke hearts,
    drained

Drain tuna and flake. Chop artichokes. Combine and mix with enough mayonnaise to moisten. Serves 4.

Optional: Stir in slivered almonds.
Optional: Substitute cubed chicken breast for tuna.

STRAWBERRY-BANANA WHIP

1 (3 oz.) pkg. strawberry Jell-O   2 sliced bananas
1 (8 oz.) Cool Whip

Prepare Jell-O with 1 cup boiling water and stir until dissolved. Add ½ cup cold water. Mix well. Chill until partially set.

Whip Jell-O, then mix in whipped cream and beat until creamy. Stir in sliced bananas. Chill until firm. Serves 4.

LIME JELLO SALAD

1 (3 oz.) pkg. lime Jell-O   1 (15 oz.) can crushed pineapple,
1 c. cottage cheese   drained

Dissolve Jell-O in 1 cup boiling water. Stir in ½ cup cold water; chill until partially set. Stir in pineapple and cottage cheese. Refrigerate until firm. Serves 4.

CUCUMBER SALAD

2 cucumbers, sliced, peeled,   Heinz cider vinegar
   seeded   1 sliced red onion

Combine; mix and chill. Serves 4.
Optional: Mix sliced cucumbers with sour cream instead of vinegar.

PISTACHIO SALAD

1 (20 oz.) can crushed pineapple   1 (3½ oz.) pkg. instant pistachio
   (undrained)   pudding mix (dry)
1 (12 oz.) Cool Whip

Combine and mix all ingredients together. Chill 2 to 3 hours before serving.
Optional: Add chopped nuts or maraschino cherries, if desired. Serves 4 to 6.

ROGENE'S CHERRY BERRY SALAD

1 (6 oz.) pkg. cherry Jell-O   1 (15 oz.) can whole berry
1 (10 oz.) pkg. frozen   cranberry sauce
   strawberries

Dissolve Jell-O as package directs in two cups boiling water, mixing well. Stir in undrained strawberries and whole berry cranberry sauce. Pour into 7x11 inch glass dish and refrigerate until set. Serves 8 to 10.
Optional: Frost firm geletin with sour cream.

FROZEN FRUIT SALAD

1 large can chunky fruit, drained   2 (3 oz.) pkg. cream cheese,
1 c. marshmallow cream   softened

Blend together cream cheese and marshmallow cream. Stir in fruit; freeze. Cut into squares. Serves 6.

BING CHERRY SALAD

1 c. pitted Bing cherries, drained   1 (3 oz.) pkg. cherry Jell-O
  (reserve juice)   1 c. crushed pineapple, drained

Prepare Jell-O with 1 cup boiling water. Stir in drained reserved juice. Chill until partially set. Mix in Bing cherries and 1 cup pineapple. Chill until firm. Serves 4 to 6.

PINEAPPLE BOATS

1 fresh pineapple   1 can tropical fruit salad, drained
2 Tbsp. shredded coconut

Cut fresh pineapple in half, leaves and all. Remove core and fruit, leaving ½ inch thick shell. Reserve pineapple.

Fill with a can of drained tropical fruit, mixed with reserved pineapple. Sprinkle coconut over top. Serves 2.

ORANGE SALAD

1 (3 oz.) pkg. orange Jell-O   1 can mandarin oranges, drained
1 c. sour cream

Prepare Jell-O according to package directions. Chill until partially set. Stir in sour cream and then add the oranges. Return to refrigerator until firm. Serves 4.

LAYERED RASPBERRY-CRANBERRY SALAD

2 (3 oz.) pkg. raspberry Jell-O   1 can whole berry cranberries
1 c. sour cream

Prepare Jell-O according to package directions; chill until partially thickened. Stir in cranberry sauce. Pour half the mixture in a dish and chill until firm in freezer. Spread sour cream over it. Top with remaining berry-Jell-O mixture which had been setting at room temperature. Chill until firm. Serves 8.

PEACH AND COTTAGE CHEESE SALAD

1 c. cottage cheese   1 can peaches (halves or slices),
2 maraschino cherries   drained

Place a scoop of cottage cheese on a lettuce leaf in center of a salad plate, surrounded by peaches. Place a maraschino cherry on top of cottage cheese as a garnish. (This is my husband's favorite salad.) Serves 2.

WILMA'S CRAN-APPLE SALAD

1 (3 oz.) pkg. orange Jell-O   1 (16 oz.) can whole berry
2 chopped apples   cranberry sauce

Prepare orange Jell-O as package directs, using 1 cup boiling water. Stir until well dissolved. Cool. Add can whole berry cranberry sauce and 2 chopped apples. Mix well. Cover and refrigerate until firm. Serves 6.

BROCCOLI RICE CASSEROLE

1 (10 oz.) box frozen chopped   1 c. cooked rice
   broccoli   1 small jar Cheez Whiz

Cook broccoli according to package directions. Cook rice according to package directions.

Combine broccoli, rice and Cheez Whiz. Mix well. Pour into greased casserole dish and bake at 350°F. for 20 to 30 minutes. Serves 6.

CAVIAR POTATOES

4 to 6 baking potatoes   1 (8 oz.) ctn. sour cream
1 jar caviar

Bake potatoes at 400°F. for an hour or until done.

Split potatoes and serve with a dollop of sour cream. Top with a spoonful of caviar. Serves 4 to 6.

ONION RICE CASSEROLE

1 (10¾ oz.) can onion soup   1 c. rice (not instant)
1 c. water

Combine soup, rice and water. Mix well and cook in a covered saucepan over medium heat for 25 minutes or until the rice is tender. Fluff with a fork. Serves 4.

CABBAGE CASSEROLE

1 head cabbage, washed and   1 c. shredded Cheddar cheese
   cooked
1 (10¾ oz.) can cream of chicken
   soup

In a buttered casserole dish, make alternate layers of cabbage, soup, and cheese. Repeat layers. Bake at 350°F. for 30 minutes. Serves 4 to 6.

MAXINE McNEIL'S ORANGE CARROTS

1 Tbsp. butter or margarine
1 Tbsp. orange marmalade

1 (15 oz.) can sliced carrots, drained

Combine butter and marmalade in a small sauce pan and heat until melted, stirring often. Add drained carrots; stir and heat until hot and glazed. Serves 4.

BROCCOLI-CAULIFLOWER CASSEROLE

1 large pkg. frozen broccoli and cauliflower

Velveeta cheese or Cheez Whiz
Salted water

Boil vegetables in salted water; drain. Add cheese and mix well. Serves 6 to 8.

GREEN BEAN CASSEROLE

1 (16 oz.) can green beans, drained
1 (10 oz.) can mushroom soup

1 small can French fried onion rings

Combine beans, soup and ½ can onion rings. Mix well. Pour into a greased baking dish and bake at 350°F. for 25 minutes. Top with remaining onion rings and bake 10 minutes longer. Serves 4 to 6.

SCALLOPED ONIONS

6 onions, peeled and sliced
3 c. crushed potato chips

1 small box Velveeta cheese

Boil onions until limp and transparent. Butter a casserole dish and layer onions alternately with cheese and potato chips. Repeat layers 1 to 2 times. Bake 20 minutes at 350°F. (This is my favorite!) Serves 6.

FRIED CABBAGE

1 cabbage, shredded
1 small onion, chopped

Vegetable oil or bacon drippings

Fry cabbage and onions in bacon drippings until tender and transparent.
Optional: Stir crumbled fried bacon into cabbage. Serves 4 to 6.

EGGPLANT CASSEROLE

1 eggplant, sliced thin (peeled)   2 sliced tomatoes
1 to 2 sliced onions

Grease a casserole dish with olive oil. Make alternate layers of eggplant, onions, and tomatoes. Repeat layers until vegetables are gone. Season to taste. Bake at 350°F. for 45 minutes. Serves 4 to 6.

MEN'S FAVORITE GREEN BEANS

2 (16 oz.) cans green beans,   Pimiento, chopped fine
   drained   1 (8 oz.) jar Kraft Cheez Whiz

Combine, mix and heat thoroughly. Serves 6.
Mrs. Manning, who gave me the recipe, assured me that men love this!

CORN-ON-THE COB

4 husked ears of corn   Butter
Salt

Drop washed, husked corn into hot boiling water. Cover; let water boil again. Turn off heat and let set 5 minutes or until tender. Serve with butter and salt. Serves 4.

CHEEZY GREEN PEAS

1 (16 oz.) can green peas   1 small jar Kraft Cheez Whiz
3 Tbsp. chopped onion

Combine peas, onions and cheese. Mix well and heat thoroughly. (Can be heated in microwave or baked 15 minutes at 325°F.) Serves 4.
Note: For a different taste, try jalapeno flavored Cheez Whiz. Very good!

GREEN BEANS ALMONDINE

1 (16 oz.) can French style green   ½ c. slivered almonds
   beans, drained
1 (10¾ oz.) can cream of celery
   soup

Combine beans, soup and almonds. Mix well and pour into a greased baking dish. Bake, uncovered, at 375°F. for 15 to 20 minutes. Serves 4 to 6.

FRIED ONION RINGS

2 onions, sliced
Enough water or milk to make a
   batter

Pancake mix

Separate sliced onions into rings. Mix together the pancake mix and water (or milk if directions call for it). Dip onion rings into batter. Fry in deep oil until golden brown. Serves 2 to 4.

SWEET POTATO CUPS

4 oranges
Miniature marshmallows

Mashed sweet potatoes

Bake sweet potatoes and mash. Season to taste.

Cut oranges in halves. Remove all fruit or ream out oranges with a juicer. (Stir oranges into potatoes - optional.)

Fill orange cups with mashed sweet potatoes. Top each potato with marshmallows and bake at 350°F. until they are melted and browned. Serves 8.

PECAN RICE PILAF

1 pkg. wild rice
3 Tbsp. margarine

½ c. pecan halves

Saute pecan halves in melted oleo. Prepare wild rice according to package directions. Stir pecans into rice. Serve hot with chicken.

FRIED GREEN TOMATOES

2 to 3 green tomatoes, sliced
½ c. flour

1 beaten egg

Dip tomato slices in flour and fry in oil.

Or, dip tomato slices in a beaten egg, then dip in flour on both sides. Fry in vegetable oil.

Or, optional: Dip tomato slices in corn meal and fry. Serves 4.

HOMINY CASSEROLE

2 (16 oz.) cans hominy, drained
1 (10 oz.) can Ro-Tel tomatoes

½ c. Cheddar cheese, grated

Combine hominy and tomatoes in saucepan. Simmer for a few minutes to cook up some of the liquid and allow flavors to blend. Pour

into casserole dish and top with cheese. Bake in 325° oven for 20 minutes, or until cheese melts. Serves 6 to 8.

Main Dishes

Hints for Meats

- Heat the frying pan before adding oil or butter to prevent sticking.
- Sprinkle salt in the bottom of a frying pan to prevent food from sticking.
- When you want a crisp, brown crust on chicken, rub mayonnaise over it.
- Try basting meat loaf with 1/2 cup brown sugar, 1 tablespoon dry mustard, 1/2 cup tomato juice, 1 1/2 cups chili sauce, and 1/2 cup pineapple juice for a delicious flavor.
- Grate an apple into hamburger, then shape into patties to add moistness.
- A large roast or turkey can be carved easily after it stands for 30 minutes.
- To remove the wild flavor, soak game birds 3 hours in 1 tablespoon baking soda and 1 tablespoon salt to 1 gallon of water. Basting in 7-Up helps take away the game taste.
- Add leftover coffee to ham, beef or pork gravy for a beautiful color.
- Use a small amount of baking powder in gravy if it seems greasy. The grease will disappear.
- Use an ice cream dipper to make meat balls.
- To make a fluffy meat loaf, beat an egg white stiff, and add it after all other ingredients have been mixed.
- When making hamburgers, mix a little flour with the meat and they will stay together better.
- For smooth brown gravy, brown the flour well in meat drippings before adding the liquid. Another way to brown flour is by placing it in a custard cup beside meat in oven. When meat is done, the flour will be brown and ready to make a nice, brown gravy.
- Raw meats, especially liver, grind easily if frozen, not stone hard, but just firm.
- To prevent splashing when frying meat, sprinkle a little salt into the pan before putting the fat in.
- The odor from baking or boiling salmon may be eliminated by squeezing lemon juice on both sides of each salmon steak or on the cut surface of the salmon, and letting it stand in the refrigerator for one hour before cooking.

BACON:
- Bacon will lie flat in the pan if you prick it thoroughly with a fork as it fries.
- Bacon dipped in flour will not shrink, or pinch a fold in the middle of a bacon slice to help prevent curling. Soaking in ice water a few minutes also works.
- A quick way to separate frozen bacon: Heat a spatula over the stove burner, then slide it under each slice to separate it from the others.

MAIN DISHES

PEPSI HAM

1 (10 to 12 lb.) cooked boneless   2 c. Pepsi-Cola
   ham
Whole cloves

    Score a cooked boneless ham. Stud with whole cloves. Place ham in a roaster. Pour 1 cup Pepsi over it. Cover tightly with lid or foil. Bake 2 hours at 325°F. Baste occasionally with the second cup of Pepsi. Serves 20.

ROAST TURKEY

Turkey (12 to 16 lb.)   Melted margarine
Salt

    Rinse turkey and pat dry with paper towels after removing giblets and neck; salt. Place turkey, breast side up, on rack in roasting pan. Baste occasionally with melted margarine. Put a tent of foil over the turkey. Roast at 325°F. for 3½ to 5 hours for 12 to 16 pound turkey. Remove foil during the last ½ hour to brown. Turkey is done when you can "shake its leg." Serves about 20 to 24.

MUSHROOM STEAK

1 round steak (2 lb.)   1 small can sliced mushrooms,
1 (10¾ oz.) can mushroom soup   drained

    Place a round steak in a 9x13 inch pan lined with foil. Pour 1 can mushroom soup over steak and top with 1 small can drained, sliced mushrooms. Cover with foil. Bake 1 hour or until tender at 350°F. Serves 4 to 6.

POT ROAST WITH VEGETABLES

1 rump roast (3 to 4 lb.)   4 potatoes, peeled
2 onions

    Grease a heavy skillet or Dutch oven. Lay roast on it and sear or brown meat on medium high heat on all sides.
    Pour 2 inches of water around the meat; cover; heat on low for several hours or until tender. Season to taste.
    Add quartered potatoes and onion to the pot about one hour before roast is done. Serves 8.

SOY BRISKET

1 brisket (3 to 4 lb.)   Soy sauce
Dash of garlic salt

Poke holes in brisket. Rub soy sauce in it until brisket turns brown. Bake, covered (with foil), at 250°F. for 6 to 8 hours. Sprinkle with garlic salt. Bake until tender. Serves 6 to 8.

ONION ROAST

1 rump or chuck roast (3 lb.)   1 pkg. Lipton's dry onion soup
Dash of garlic powder   mix

Place a beef roast on a large sheet of foil. Sprinkle 1 package of Lipton's onion soup mix over the meat. Sprinkle roast with a dash of garlic powder. Seal foil.

Place in large pan and bake 3 hours at 300°F. or until tender (or bake at 200°F. for 8 to 9 hours, depending on the size of the roast). Serves 6.

CHEESE CRAB SQUARES

1 stick margarine, softened   8 oz. Kraft nippy cheese roll, soft
1 (7½ oz.) can crabmeat

Combine margarine, cheese roll and drained crabmeat. Mix well.
Remove crust from one loaf of bread. Cut each slice into 4 pieces. Spread the cheese-crab mixture on the bread. Refrigerate.

When ready to serve, place on cookie sheet with edges and heat at 450°F. until bubbly. Serves hot. Serve with salad and fruit. Serves 6 to 8.

BARBECUED PORK CHOPS

4 to 6 pork chops   1 to 2 c. Coca-Cola
1 c. catsup

Brown pork chops in greased skillet. Pour Coke and catsup over chops. Cover with lid or foil and simmer about 1½ hours or until tender. Serves 4 to 6.

CHICKEN ITALIANNE

4 chicken breasts, skinned   1 (8 oz.) bottle Italian dressing
Dash of garlic salt

Lay chicken breasts (skinned and boned) in a greased 9x13 inch pan. Pour 8 ounce bottle of Italian dressing over chicken. Sprinkle a small dash of garlic salt over it. Bake 2½ to 3 hours at 275°F. to 300°F. Serves 4.

HUSBAND'S FAVORITE FLANK STEAK

1 (2 lb.) beef flank steak   ⅓ c. Worcestershire sauce
⅓ c. soy sauce

Score flank steak with a sharp knife and place in a Pyrex dish. Combine soy sauce and Worcestershire sauce and pour marinade over steak. Marinate steak in the refrigerator for 2 to 4 hours. Turn steak several times.

Remove steak from marinade and broil or grill steak to desired doneness. Turn with tongs and broil other side. Let set 10 minutes before slicing. Slice across the grain, diagonally, into thin strips. Serves 4 to 6.

CRISPY BAKED CHICKEN

4 chicken breast halves   ½ c. evaporated milk
1 c. crushed corn flakes

Dip chicken breasts in ½ cup evaporated milk poured into a bowl. Roll chicken in a cup of corn flakes placed in a bowl.

Lay chicken in a greased 9x13 inch pan and bake 1 hour or until tender at 350°F. Serves 4.

FILET OF SOLE

4 filets of sole   1 dash of paprika (or lemon
1 (10 oz.) can cream of celery   pepper)
   soup

Lay filets of sole in a greased 9x13 inch dish. Pour one can of cream of celery soup over the fish. Bake at 350°F. for about 45 minutes or until tender. Sprinkle with paprika or lemon pepper to serve. Serves 4.

FRIED CATFISH

Catfish   Corn meal
Vegetable oil

Dip catfish in corn meal and slowly fry on low heat in a little vegetable oil until golden on both sides.

SALMON PATTIES

1 (7½ oz.) can pink salmon,   1 beaten egg
   rinsed and drained   1 c. cracker crumbs

Combine salmon, egg and crumbs. Mix well. Shape into patties and fry on both sides. Serves 4.

SAUSAGE-RICE CASSEROLE

1 lb. sausage (I prefer R.B. Rice's   3 c. cooked rice
  hot sausage)   1 can mushroom soup

    Fry sausage; crumble and drain.
    Combine and mix sausage, 3 cups cooked rice and 1 can mushroom soup together. Pour into a greased casserole dish and bake at 350°F. for 30 minutes. Serves 4.

RITZY BAKED CHICKEN

4 chicken breasts, skinned,   1 c. sour cream
  boned, and halved   1 c. crushed Ritz crackers

    Roll boneless skinned chicken breasts in sour cream, then in crushed Ritz crackers. Bake at 350°F. for 1 hour or until tender.
    Serve with rice, if desired. Serves 4.

BARBEQUED CHICKEN

4 chicken breasts, halved   1 small bottle barbeque sauce
1 (10 oz.) bottle 7-Up

    Place chicken in greased skillet. Pour barbeque sauce and 7-Up over chicken. Simmer for 1 hour or until tender. Serves 4.

QUESADILLAS

10 flour tortillas   1 to 2 c. shredded Cheddar
1 small chopped onion   cheese

    Place desired amount of cheese and onion in center of a flour tortilla. Roll up and secure with wooden picks. Fry in melted margarine on both sides until golden brown. Serves 4 to 5.

CORNISH HENS

6 Cornish hens   Wild rice, prepared according to
Lemon pepper   pkg. directions

    Wash 6 Cornish hens and pat dry with paper towels. Sprinkle with lemon pepper. Baste with oleo. Place in a large pan and roast at 350°F. until tender, about 1½ hours.
    Serve with wild rice. Serves 6 to 12.

BOILED BRISKET

3 to 4 lb. beef brisket
1 onion, quartered

2 to 3 celery stalks and tops, cut in 2 inch pieces

Place brisket in a pot with enough water to cover the meat. Add 1 quartered onion and celery tops and pieces. Cover with tight lid and simmer for 3 to 4 hours or until the meat is tender.
Serve with horseradish sauce, if desired. Serves 6 to 8.

BAKED CUBE STEAKS

4 to 6 cube steaks
2 c. water

Flour

Flour cube steaks and brown in greased skillet. Add 2 cups water and bake, covered, about 2 hours at 350°F. or until tender. Serves 4 to 6.

SPANISH MEATLOAF

1 lb. hamburger
1 can Spanish rice, drained

1 egg, beaten

Combine and mix well. Pour into a greased loaf pan. Bake about 1 hour at 350°F. Drain off excess liquid. Serves 4.
Optional: May add 1 small chopped onion.

BROILED LEMON LAMB CHOPS

8 lamb chops
¼ c. olive oil

Juice of 1 lemon and 1 tsp. grated rind

Brush lamb chops with mixture of olive oil, lemon juice and rind. Broil about 4 inches from the heat for 7 to 10 minutes on each side. Baste occasionally as the chops broil. Serves 8.

MUSHROOM-ONION ROAST

1 chuck roast (3 to 4 lb.)
1 (10¾ oz.) can mushroom soup

½ pkg. dry soup mix

Brown or sear meat on all sides. (This step can be omitted, but the roast tastes better if it is seared.)
Place roast on 2 to 3 thicknesses of foil. Spread soup over meat, then sprinkle with onion soup mix. Wrap roast tightly. Place in pan and bake at 325°F. for 3 to 4 hours or until done. Serves 6 to 8.

JUDY McDONALD HUTCHINSON'S HAM AND RED-EYE GRAVY

4 slices county ham   Strong black coffee
Hot sauce

Fry ham slices in heavy skillet, turning frequently. Remove ham slices. Add coffee to skillet (in the amount of gravy desired). Simmer, stir, and scrape. Add hot sauce to taste. Serve with ham. Serves 4.

Judy was my college roommate during my senior year and she gave me this recipe.

CHILI CASSEROLE

2 (16 oz.) cans chili con carne   1 pkg. corn chips (or Fritos)
1 c. Cheddar cheese, shredded

Place alternate layers of chili and corn chips in a greased casserole dish. Top with cheese. Cover. Bake at 350°F. for 30 minutes. Serves 6 to 8.

COCA-COLA BARBEQUED CHICKEN

4 to 6 chicken breasts or any   ½ bottle catsup
   favorite chicken part   1 (12 oz.) Coca-Cola

Skin, bone, and split chicken breasts. Place chicken in large greased skillet. Pour Coca-Cola and catsup over chicken. Cover; cook about 1 hour until tender. (Check at 30 to 45 minutes for doneness.) Serves 4 to 6.

BREAKFAST CASSEROLE

2½ c. shredded Cheddar cheese   1 c. whipping cream
6 eggs

In a buttered 10x6 inch baking dish, make a layer of 1½ cups cheese. Carefully break 6 eggs over cheese. Pierce each egg yolk. Sprinkle 1 cup shredded cheese over eggs. Pour cream over the casserole. Bake at 350°F. for 15 to 20 minutes.

Great served with bacon and toast! Serves 6.

VELMA STEWART'S RUSSIAN CHICKEN SAUCE

Sauce:
1 (8 oz.) bottle Russian salad   1 pkg. dry onion soup mix
   dressing   (Lipton's)
8 oz. jar apricot preserves

Sauce: Combine Russian dressing, dry soup mix and apricot preserves. Mix well. Pour over 6 chicken breasts in a buttered 9x13 inch dish. Bake 2 hours at 300°F. Serves 6.

HOBO DINNER

1 lb. hamburger   4 potatoes
4 onion slices

Shape hamburger into patties. Slice potatoes ½ inch thick. Place patties on square of foil. Top with potato slices (2 to 3), then a slice of onion. Season to taste. Fold tightly; place in pan and bake 45 minutes at 350°F. Serves 4.

CROWN ROAST PORK

6 to 8 lb. (20 ribs) pork loin   Crab apples (small)
Parsley

Ask your butcher to make the crown from 2 strips of pork loin containing about 20 ribs. Remove backbone. Season to taste.
Place roast in roasting pan, bone ends up. Wrap bone ends in foil. Roast, uncovered, at 325°F. for 2 to 3 hours, or until well done and tender.
To serve, replace foil wraps with crab apples or paper frills. Garnish platter with parsley. Serves 10.

SAUCY HADDOCK FILLETS

1 lb. haddock fillets (thawed, if   1 can cream of celery soup
  frozen)   1 c. shredded Cheddar cheese

Drain and blot fillets with paper towels. Arrange fish in a greased 9x13 inch dish. Pour soup evenly over fish. Sprinkle cheese over soup. Bake at 350°F. until done. Serves 4.

MOCK FILLET MIGNON

1 to 2 lb. ground round steak   ½ pkg. dry onion soup mix
Bacon   (Lipton's)

Combine ground round and onion soup mix. Shape into thick patties. Wrap a slice of bacon around each and secure with wooden picks. Place in 9x13 inch oven dish and bake at 450°F. for 15 to 20 minutes OR broil on each side.
Good with sauteed mushrooms. Serves 4 to 6.

PORK CHOPS AND RICE

4 pork chops   1 box long grain and wild rice
1 (10 oz.) can Golden Mushroom
  soup

Brown chops on both sides. Combine soup with ¾ can water and the rice package ingredients in a saucepan; heat thoroughly. Pour over chops in a skillet and simmer for an hour or until tender. Serves 4.

SCALLOPED OYSTERS

1 to 2 cans oysters, drained   ¼ c. melted oleo
  (reserve liquid)   Cracker crumbs

Cover bottom of a buttered casserole dish with a layer of buttered crumbs. Top with oysters. Repeat layers 2 to 3 times.

Pour milk and reserved liquid from oysters over casserole until crackers are well soaked. Sprinkle crumbs over top and bake at 350° for 1 hour or until browned. Serves 4 to 6.

MOUTTET'S CHICKEN

4 chicken breasts   1½ c. shredded Cheddar cheese
1 (10¾ oz.) can mushroom soup

Skin and bone chicken, then place it in a greased 9x13 inch pan and bake for 1 hour at 350°F.

Remove from oven and spread soup over chicken. Top with cheese. Bake ½ hour longer (more or less). Serves 4.

OVERNIGHT BRISKET

1 brisket (3 to 4 lb.)   2 Tbsp. liquid smoke
Garlic salt

Rub 2 tablespoons liquid smoke on the sides of brisket. Sprinkle with garlic salt. Wrap tightly in foil. Refrigerate overnight.

Next day: Sprinkle with more garlic salt. Rewrap in foil. Bake in 9x13 inch dish (or whatever size is needed) for 6 hours at 250°F. or at 325°F. for 5 hours.

Refrigerate overnight again. Next day, slice. If desired, pour barbecue sauce over it and reheat. Serves 6 to 8.

CORY RIGGS' BAR-B-QUE BEEF

1 lb. ground sirloin or hamburger   16 oz. bar-b-que sauce (your
½ c. brown sugar   choice)

Brown, crumble, and drain the meat. Stir in brown sugar and bar-b-que sauce. Cover and simmer for 15 minutes, stirring often.

Spoon onto heated hamburger buns. Serves 4 to 6

SPEEDY SPAGHETTI

1 lb. pkg. spaghetti
1 lb. hamburger
1 (32 oz.) jar Ragu chunky garden
   style spaghetti sauce (with
   extra tomatoes, garlic and
   onions)

Prepare spaghetti according to package directions. Brown meat; crumble and drain. Stir spaghetti sauce into the meat and heat thoroughly. Pour drained spaghetti into a large platter and spread meat sauce over it. Or Combine spaghetti and meat sauce and mix thoroughly. Serves 4.

Optional: Top with 1 cup shredded Cheddar cheese and heat at 350° until cheese is melted.

MACARONI AND CHEESE

1 pkg. macaroni, cooked
   according to package
   directions
12 oz. shredded (or cubed)
   Cheddar cheese

1 (16 oz.) can whole tomatoes,
   drained and chopped
   (reserve juice)

In a greased 2 quart casserole, make alternating layers of macaroni, cheese, and tomatoes. Repeat layers. Pour reserved tomato juice over top. Dot with margarine. Bake at 350°F. for one hour. Serves 4 to 6.

CHEESE GRITS

1 c. hominy grits (quick grits)
1 c. Cheddar cheese, shredded

1 beaten egg

Prepare grits according to package directions. Stir shredded cheese and beaten egg into grits. (Optional: Stir in 2 tablespoons margarine.)

Cook in saucepan over low heat until cheese melts. Mix and pour into a 1½ to 2 quart buttered casserole dish. Bake for 30 minutes at 350°F. or until golden brown. Serves 4.

Breads
Rolls
Pastries

Hints for Breads

- To avoid lumps in bread batter, add a pinch of salt to the flour before it is wet.
- When cool-rise dough "rests", the resting takes the place of the first rising in other methods.
- Overkneading may cause large air holes in the crust.
- A small dish of water in the oven while baking bread will keep it from getting a hard crust.
- When making rolls, add only enough flour to keep dough from sticking to your hands or the board. Keep the dough as soft as possible.
- After rolls have baked, remove from pan immediately to prevent steam from forming and making them heavy.
- Brush rolls with one beaten egg and 1/4 cup water before baking. Sprinkle with sesame seed, poppy seed, etc., for that professional look.
- Let nut breads and other quick breads stand for 10 minutes before removing from the pan to allow them to become firmer. Do not cool completely in the pan or they will become soggy.
- For tender muffins, mix liquid and dry ingredients until just moistened. Overmixing causes muffins to be tough, coarse-textured, and full of tunnels.
- Use the divider from an ice tray to cut biscuits in a hurry. Shape dough to conform with size of divider and cut. After baking, biscuits will separate at dividing lines.
- Kneading the dough for a half minute after mixing improves the texture of baking powder biscuits.
- Use cooking or salad oil in waffles and hotcakes instead of shortening. No extra pan or bowl to melt the shortening and no waiting.
- A rib of celery in your bread bag will keep the bread fresh for a longer time.
- Freshen dry bread by wrapping in a damp towel and placing it in the refrigerator for 24 hours. Remove towel and heat in oven for a few minutes.
- Put frozen bread loaves in a clean brown paper bag and place in 325° oven for 5 minutes to thaw completely.
- Substitutes that can be used for bread crumbs are dry cereal and potato flakes.
- Cut "figure eight" yeast rolls with a doughnut cutter. Pick up the ring, stretch it, then twist. No ends to tuck under and a pretty roll for the pastry or bread platter.
- To raise bread dough in your oven, preheat the oven at lowest possible setting for 10 minutes. Turn the oven off and then put in mixing bowl of dough, covered.

BREADS, ROLLS, PASTRIES

ICE CREAM MUFFINS

2 c. self-rising flour   Margarine or butter
1 pt. vanilla ice cream

Blend together flour and ice cream until well moistened. The batter will be lumpy. Fill 10 well-buttered muffin cups ¾ full and bake at 350°F. for 20 minutes. Serves 5 to 10.

MEXICAN CORN BREAD

1 (8½ oz.) pkg. Jiffy corn bread   1 small can cream-style corn
   mix   ½ c. shredded Cheddar cheese

Prepare corn bread according to package directions. Stir in corn and ¼ cup shredded cheese. Pour into a greased skillet or muffin tins. Top with remaining ¼ cup cheese. Bake at 400°F. for 15 to 20 minutes. Serves 4.

MAYONNAISE ROLLS

2 c. self-rising flour   4 Tbsp. mayonnaise
1 c. milk

Combine, mix and pour into greased muffin tins. Bake at 400°F. for 22 minutes. Serves 6 to 8.

HOT CHEESY SLICES

½ lb. grated Cheddar cheese
1 c. mayonnaise
4 to 6 sourdough French rolls, cut
   in ¼ inch slices (or French
   bread could be used)

Mix together cheese and mayonnaise. Spread on bread slices. Place bread on cookie sheet and bake 8 to 10 minutes at 350°F.
For variety, sometimes I mix 2 cheeses, Cheddar and Swiss, with mayonnaise and spread on the bread. Serves 4 to 6.

POPOVERS

4 eggs   2 c. milk
2 c. flour

Beat eggs; add milk, then flour. Mix well. Fill greased muffin tins ¾ full and bake at 450°F. for 25 minutes. Reduce heat to 350°F. for 15 to 20 minutes more. (Some stoves may cook faster.) Serves 6.

SOUR CREAM ROLLS

1 c. sour cream
½ c. melted margarine

1 c. self-rising flour

Combine flour, oleo, and sour cream; mix. Pour into greased miniature muffin tins and bake at 450°F. for 15 minutes. Serves 4.

MINI CINNAMON ROLLS

Margarine
Brown sugar

1 pkg. Pillsbury crescent rolls

In greased miniature muffin pans, place ½ teaspoon margarine and ½ teaspoon brown sugar in each cup.

Take 1 package Pillsbury crescent rolls and roll out. Take 2 squares; press together the creases. Roll up tightly. Slice each roll in 6 slices. Lay a slice in each muffin cup on top of oleo and brown sugar. Bake at 375°F. for 10 to 12 minutes. Serves 6.

SHORTBREAD

4 c. flour
1 lb. butter

1 c. brown sugar

Mix flour and sugar. Cut in butter with pastry blender until mixture is the size of green peas. Pat mixture into a rimmed jelly roll pan. Bake at 325°F. for 40 minutes. Cut into small squares. Turn off oven and place in oven for 10 minutes. Serves 12 or more.

SPEEDY BANANA PIE

2 to 3 sliced bananas
1 baked, cooled pie crust

1 (4 oz.) box prepared banana
   pudding

Place banana slices in cooled crust. Pour pudding over bananas. Garnish with banana slices. Let stand 5 to 10 minutes. Serves 6.

Optional: For a speedy meringue, sprinkle 2 cups miniature marshmallows over top of pie and broil 2 to 3 minutes until light brown and partially melted.

CHOCOLATE ALMOND PIE

1 (8 oz.) Hershey's chocolate
   almond bar
1 small tub Cool Whip

1 (8 inch) graham cracker
   prepared crust

Melt Hershey's bar in top of a double boiler. Cool. Stir Cool Whip into chocolate. Fill the pie crust and chill.

Garnish, if desired, by using a potato peeler to shave chocolate curls off a Hershey's candy bar. Serves 6 to 8.

FROZEN LEMONADE PIE

1 small can frozen pink
   lemonade (or limeade)
1 small ctn. Cool Whip

1 (14 oz.) can Eagle Brand
   condensed, sweetened milk

Combine lemonade, Cool Whip and Eagle Brand milk. Mix well; chill. Serve as pudding or pour into a pie crust (graham cracker) and freeze. Serves 6 to 8.

CHERRY COBBLER

1 (21 oz.) can Wilderness cherry
   pie filling
1 to 2 sticks margarine, sliced

1 box yellow or white cake mix
   (dry)

Spread cherry pie filling in a greased 9x13 inch baking dish. Sprinkle with cake mix. Top with slices of margarine. Bake at 350°F. for about 35 minutes. Delicious served with a dip of vanilla ice cream. Serves 8.

Note: Any pie filling or canned fruit could be substituted for the cherries.

STRAWBERRY PIE

1 (3 oz.) pkg. strawberry Jell-O
1 pt. vanilla ice cream

1 pt. fresh or frozen strawberries

Prepare Jell-O with 1 cup boiling water. Mix well until Jell-O is dissolved. Stir in the ice cream, then the berries. Chill and serve as pudding or pour into a prepared pie crust. Serves 6.

SHAKER LEMON PIE

2 lemons, sliced thin (rind and
   all)

1½ c. sugar
4 eggs

Place lemon slices in a bowl; pour sugar over them. Mix well and let stand 2 to 3 hours.

Beat 4 eggs and pour over lemons. Fill an uncooked pie crust. Add a top crust. Make vents in top crust. Bake at 450°F. for 15 minutes. Reduce heat to 350°F. and bake until done. Serves 8.

Cakes
Cookies
Desserts

Dessert Hints

• Add confectioners' sugar to whipping cream before beating. The whipped cream stands up well even if it is not used immediately.

• To make powdered sugar, blend 1 cup granulated sugar and 1 tablespoon cornstarch in the blender at medium speed for 2 minutes.

• To add a delightful flavor to whipped cream, add a teaspoon of strained honey or maple syrup instead of sugar. It will remain firm all day.

• Whipping cream retains its shape if when whipping you add 1/2 to 1 teaspoon of light corn syrup per half pint of cream.

• Add a tablespoon of powdered orange-flavored drink mix, such as Tang, to a cup of whipped topping for a flavorful, different taste. Good over gingerbread or pumpkin pie.

• Soak peeled apples in cold water to which 1 teaspoon of salt has been added. They will not discolor.

• A tasty sauce for baked apples can be made by mixing honey and whipped cream.

• Substitute 3/4 cup honey for 1 cup of sugar up to 1 cup total.

• When using honey, reduce the total amount of other liquids by 1/4 cup per cup of honey in the conventional recipe.

• Reduce baking temperature 25° to prevent over-browning when cooking with honey.

• To melt chocolate, grease the pan in which it is to be melted.

• A pinch of salt added to very sour fruits while cooking will greatly reduce the amount of sugar needed.

• Keep apples, bananas, pears and other fruits from discoloring when cut-up by coating them with orange juice or diluted lemon juice.

CAKES, COOKIES, DESSERTS

PINEAPPLE CAKE

1 (20 oz.) can pineapple, crushed
2 sticks margarine, sliced

1 box white or yellow cake mix

Spread pineapple in a greased 9x13 inch dish. Sprinkle dry cake mix over the fruit. Dot with slices of oleo. Bake at 350°F. for about 35 minutes or until browned. Serves 6 to 8.

Optional: Top with a dip of vanilla ice cream.

PUDDING CAKE

1 cake mix (any flavor)
1 pkg. Dream Whip, prepared

1 (3 oz.) pkg. pudding (any flavor)

Prepare cake according to package directions and bake. Cool completely.

Prepare Dream Whip as package directs (or use Cool Whip).

Spread pudding between cake layers. Frost with the whipped Dream Whip cream. Serves 8.

BAKED ALASKA

8 brownies (or squares of cake)
Strawberry ice cream

Meringue (prepared according to a meringue recipe)

Spread ice cream on top of cake or brownie, then spread meringue over everything, covering entire surface and sealing edges.

Place individual Baked Alaskas on a jelly roll pan and bake at 500°F. for 5 minutes or until lightly browned. Serves 8.

GERMAN CHOCOLATE CAKE

1 pkg. German chocolate cake mix
1 (9 or 12 oz.) pkg. Cool Whip topping

1 pkg. German chocolate frosting mix

Prepare cake as package directs and bake in 2 layers. Slice horizontally to make 4 layers.

Combine and mix frosting with Cool Whip. Use to frost each layer and cover cake with frosting. Serves 8.

WALNUT CAKE

1 pkg. yellow cake mix
1 c. pancake syrup

1 c. chopped black walnuts

Prepare cake according to package directions. Stir in nuts and pour into a buttered 9x13 inch pan. Pour syrup over batter. Do not stir. Bake according to package directions.
Serve warm. Top with whipped cream, if desired. Serves 9.

ANGEL PUDDING CAKE

1 angel food cake, cubed
1 pkg. chocolate pudding

1 (8 to 12 oz.) container Cool Whip topping

Place cake cubes in a greased 9x13 inch pan or glass Pyrex dish.
Prepare pudding according to package directions and spread over cake cubes.
Spread Cool Whip over pudding. Refrigerate 6 hours. Cut into squares to serve. Serves 9.

STRAWBERRY SHORTCAKE

1 pound cake, sliced in 12 slices
1 pt. strawberries, sliced and sweetened

1 small container Cool Whip topping

Place 6 cake slices on six dessert plates. Arrange half the strawberries over the cake slices. Repeat layers. Top with whipped cream. Serves 6.

LEMON CHEESECAKE

1 (4 oz.) pkg. instant lemon pudding mix
1 graham cracker crust, baked

8 oz. Philadelphia cream cheese, softened

Prepare pudding as directed, except blend cream cheese with milk before stirring into pudding. Pour into a baked crust and chill 2 to 4 hours. Serves 6.

CRUSTLESS CHEESE CAKE

3 eggs
⅔ c. sugar

2 (8 oz.) pkg. cream cheese

Combine and mix with an electric mixer. Pour into a buttered glass pie pan and bake 30 minutes at 350°F. Cool. Keep refrigerated.
This can be cut into wedges and served plain, or topped with cherry or blueberry pie filling, if desired. Serves 6 to 8.

ANN'S CHOCOLATE CHERRY CAKE

1 box Duncan Hines devils food cake mix	1 (21 oz.) can cherry pie filling 2 eggs

Combine and mix cake mix and eggs. Stir in cherry pie filling. Mix until well blended. Pour into a greased and floured 9x13 inch pan and bake for 35 to 40 minutes at 350°F.

For 2 (9 inch) cake pans, bake for 25 to 35 minutes. For Bundt pan, bake for 40 to 50 minutes.

Frost as desired. Serves 8.

PEANUT BUTTER COOKIES

1 (14 oz.) can Eagle Brand sweetened milk	½ c. chunky peanut butter ½ c. chopped nuts

Mix and drop by teaspoonfuls on greased and floured cookie sheets. Bake 7 to 9 minutes at 375°F. to 400°F. Makes about 36 cookies. Serves 10 to 12.

RITZY CHOCOLATE COOKIES

1 box Ritz crackers Chunky peanut butter	1 (12 oz.) pkg. chocolate chips

Spread a layer of peanut butter on each Ritz cracker.

Melt chocolate chips in top of a double boiler over boiling water. Stir until smooth.

Dip crackers in chocolate. Be sure to completely cover the peanut butter with chocolate. Lay on waxed paper to cool.

MACAROONS

1 (14 oz.) pkg. shredded coconut 1 (14 oz.) can Eagle Brand milk	1 tsp. vanilla

Combine and mix all ingredients. Drop by spoonfuls onto a greased cookie sheet. Bake 8 minutes at 375°F. Cool before removing from pan. Makes about 3 dozen.

HONEY WAFER COOKIES

3 egg whites ½ c. honey	1 c. graham cracker crumbs

Beat egg whites until stiff. Gradually mix in ½ cup honey. Stir in 1 cup graham cracker crumbs. Drop by teaspoonfuls onto well greased cookie sheets. Bake at 300°F. for about 8 minutes. Makes 2 to 3 dozen.

KAREN'S CHOCOLATE - PEANUT BUTTER TARTS

1 roll refrigerated ready-to-slice
  peanut butter cookie dough
  or sugar cookie dough

2 pkg. Reese's bite-size peanut
  butter cups
Melted butter

Slice cookie dough in 1 inch slices, then quarter the slices. Lay one piece in each miniature muffin tin (greased well with melted butter). Bake 8 minutes at 350°F. While cookies are hot and puffed, gently push a peanut butter cup into the center of each cookie. Cool; remove from tins. Keep refrigerated. Makes 32 to 36.

Variation: Use Chocolate Chip Cookie dough.

MIRACLE PEANUT BUTTER COOKIES

1 c. chunky or extra chunky Peter
  Pan peanut butter

1 egg
1 c. sugar

Combine peanut butter, sugar and egg. Mix well. Shape into balls. Flatten and criss-cross with fork dipped in sugar. Bake on greased cookie sheet for 8 to 10 minutes at 375°F. Yield: 3 dozen.

M & M PARTY MIX

M&M's
Peanuts

Popcorn (or raisins)

Combine M&M's, peanuts and popcorn. (If preferred, substitute raisins for popcorn.)

CHOCOLATE CHIP BARS

2 c. crushed graham crackers
1 c. chocolate chips

1 can Eagle Brand sweetened
  milk

Combine and mix well all ingredients. Spread in a greased 9x9 inch pan. Bake at 350°F. for 20 to 25 minutes. Cut into bars. Serves 9 to 12.

PEANUT CLUSTERS

1½ lb. almond bark
1 (9 oz.) pkg. salted peanuts

1 (12 oz.) pkg. chocolate chips

Melt 1½ pounds almond bark and 12 ounces chocolate chips together in the top of a double boiler over boiling water. Stir constantly. When melted and smooth, stir in the peanuts. Drop by spoonfuls onto waxed paper. Let set until firm, or chill.

OREO COOKIE ICE CREAM

½ gal. vanilla ice cream, softened   1 small pkg. Oreo cookies,
12 oz. Cool Whip   crushed

Mix together and freeze in a 9x13 inch pan. Cut into squares to serve. Serves 9.

MERINGUE SHELLS

3 egg whites   ¼ tsp. cream of tartar
1 c. sugar

Beat egg whites and cream of tartar until frothy. Beat in sugar, one tablespoon at a time, until very stiff and glossy. Spread on heavy brown paper on a cookie sheet in 8 individual round or heart shapes (or spread in one large round shape). Build up sides and shape with back of a spoon.
Heat oven to 275°F. and bake one hour. Turn off oven and let it set in the oven until it is cool.
Fill with choice of pudding, cherry pie filling or ice cream. Top with sauce (optional). Serves 8.

PEANUT BUTTER PIE

¾ c. chunky peanut butter   1 graham cracker crust (or
1 qt. vanilla ice cream, softened   chocolate crust)

Combine peanut butter and softened ice cream. Mix well. Pour into your choice of pie crust and freeze. Serves 6 to 8.

ORANGE PINEAPPLE SHERBET

1 (20 oz.) can crushed pineapple   2 cans (14 oz.) Eagle Brand
   (undrained)   sweetened milk
1 large bottle Orange Crush (2
   liter bottle)

Combine and mix all ingredients. Freeze. Serves 8.

YOGURT PIE

16 oz. strawberry yogurt   9 inch graham cracker crust or an
8 oz. Cool Whip   Oreo chocolate crust

Combine and mix yogurt and whipped cream. Pour into crust and freeze. Garnish with fresh strawberries, if desired. Serves 6 to 8.

CHOCOLATE SANDWICHES

Graham cracker squares
Hershey's chocolate squares

Marshmallows, partially melted

Place graham cracker squares on a jelly roll pan. Top with a square of Hershey's chocolate. Lay a hot marshmallow over chocolate, then place a second cracker over marshmallow to form a sandwich.

CHOCOLATE MILK SHAKE

4 c. milk
8 Tbsp. chocolate syrup

4 scoops vanilla ice cream

Combine in blender the ice cream, chocolate syrup and 1 cup milk. Gradually add more milk and blend until smooth. Pour into tall glasses. Serves 4.

SCOTCH SHORTBREAD

⅓ c. sugar
3 c. flour

½ lb. butter (not oleo)

Cream together butter and sugar. Mix in flour. Mixture will be stiff and crumbly. Press it into a square 8 inch pan and bake about an hour at 300°F. Serves 9.

FORGOTTEN MINT PUFFS

3 egg whites
⅔ c. sugar

1 c. mint chocolate chips

Beat egg whites to stiff peaks. Gradually add sugar, beating after each addition. Stir in mint flavored chocolate chips. Drop by teaspoonfuls onto greased cookie sheet.

Preheat oven to 375°F. Place puffs in oven. Turn off heat immediately. Forget puffs and leave them in the oven overnight. Do not peek inside oven. Puffs will be ready the next day. Makes about 3 dozen.

CHOCOLATE CHEERIOS

2 c. chocolate chips
3 c. plain Cheerios

¾ c. chunky peanut butter

Melt chocolate chips in double boiler. Mix in the peanut butter. Stir until smooth. Stir in Cheerios. Drop by spoonfuls onto waxed paper and let set until firm.

CHINESE NOODLE CANDY

1 (12 oz.) pkg. chocolate chips   ½ c. chopped pecans
1 can Chinese noodles

Melt chocolate. Stir in Chinese noodles and nuts. Drop by spoonfuls onto waxed paper. Let set until they are firm.

CHOCOLATE BANANA CREPES

4 bananas   1 can Hershey's chocolate syrup
8 crepes

Split bananas lengthwise. Lay half of one banana in the middle of a crepe. Fold the crepe and drizzle chocolate syrup over it. Serves 8.

BLACKBERRY ICE CREAM

2 c. frozen blackberries   1 c. whipping cream
⅓ c. sugar

Mix cream and sugar until thickened and smooth. Add frozen black-berries ¼ cup at a time and blend in an electric mixer or a blender until smooth. Serve immediately or freeze. Serves 4.

MRS. TRUMAN'S COCONUT BALLS

1 (7 oz.) pkg. shredded coconut   ⅔ c. Eagle Brand sweetened
1 tsp. vanilla   condensed milk

Combine the 3 ingredients and mix well. Shape into balls. Bake on greased cookie sheets for 15 minutes at 350°F.
Note: Mrs. Truman served these at some White House gatherings. Makes about 3 dozen.

JIMMY CARTER FUDGE

12 oz. chocolate chips   1 (14 oz.) can Eagle Brand
12 oz. peanut butter (extra   sweetened condensed milk
   chunky)

Melt chocolate chips and peanut butter together in top of a double boiler over hot water. Remove from heat and stir in milk. Pour into an 8x8 inch pan lined with waxed paper and let it set until firm. Serves 8 to 12.

RICE KRISPIE BARS

½ lb. marshmallows   5 c. Rice Krispies
¼ c. oleo

Melt oleo and marshmallows in the top of a double boiler. Stir in cereal and mix well. Press into a buttered 9 inch square pan and cut into bars. Serves 9 to 12.

ORANGE SHERBET CUPS

4 oranges   Orange sherbet
Mint leaves

Cut oranges in halves. Hollow out the pulp. Fill the cups with orange sherbet. Garnish with a mint leaf. Serves 8.

CHEWY CHOCOLATE WALNUT DROPS

2 (1 oz.) sq. unsweetened   1 (14 oz.) can Eagle Brand
   chocolate   sweetened condensed milk
⅔ c. chopped black walnuts or
   pecans

Melt chocolate squares in double boiler over hot water. Stir in milk until well blended. Mix in nuts. Drop mixture by teaspoonfuls onto a greased baking sheet. Bake at 350°F. for 12 to 15 minutes. Makes about 3 dozen.

TURTLES

Pecan halves   Hershey's candy bars
Caramels, cut in halves

Cover pecan halves with ½ the caramel. Place in 300°F. oven until caramel melts. Remove from oven and put 1 square of Hershey's chocolate bar on top. Return to oven until chocolate melts. Let set on counter until turtles harden and meld together.

POPSICLES MIX

2 pkg. Kool-Aid (any flavor)   6 oz. pkg. Jell-O (any flavor)
1 c. sugar

Mix together Kool-Aid, Jell-O and sugar and store in a tightly closed container until ready to use.

To make popsicles: Mix 6 tablespoons dry mixture to ¾ cup boiling water. Add ¾ cup cold water. Pour into popsicle molds and freeze.

MAMA'S BANANA PUDDING DESSERT

1 box vanilla wafer cookies   4 to 6 sliced bananas
1 (3½ oz.) pkg. banana pudding

Prepare banana pudding according to package directions.

Make a cookie crust by placing whole cookies in bottom and along sides of a Pyrex dish.

Make layers of pudding, sliced bananas and cookies. Repeat layers until all ingredients have been used. Refrigerate 2 to 4 hours to blend flavors. Serves 4.

Microwave
Miscellaneous

Microwave Hints

SOFTEN:
- Lumpy brown or white sugar: Heat in microwave with a cup of boiling water.
- Cream cheese: Remove foil; heat 8-ounce package 2 minutes on LOW.
- Butter or margarine: Remove foil; heat 1 stick for 1 minute on LOW.
- Raisins in hot water: Heat 2 to 3 minutes on HIGH; let stand 2 minutes.
- Acorn squash: Cook 1 1/2 minutes on HIGH to cut in half easier.
- Citrus fruit: Heat 15 to 20 seconds before squeezing to get more juice
- Honey that has sugared.
- Almond bark: Heat 1 pound for 2 minutes on MEDIUM; stir, then cook 30 to 60 seconds more, stirring.
- Chocolate: Heat 1-ounce square for 2 to 3 minutes on LOW.

THAW:
- Whipped topping, small carton: Heat 1 minute on LOW. (Center should still be slightly firm but will blend in.) Don't overheat!
- Frozen orange juice: Remove top metal lid; heat 6-ounce can 30 seconds; 12-ounce can 45 second on HIGH.
- To toast coconut: Spread 1/2 cup in pie plate; cook 3 to 4 minutes, stirring every 30 seconds after 2 minutes. Watch closely, as it browns quickly once it starts turning brown.
- One cup herbs on a paper towel will dry in about 4 minutes. Crush and store in airtight container.
- When warming rolls, place cup of water in a corner of the microwave.
- Scald milk 2 minutes per cup, stirring once each minute.
- Heat water directly in teapot for tea.
- Don't use recycled paper products in microwave; they might ignite.
- Use a round dish instead of a square one to assure even cooking.
- Cook meat loaf in a ring. Place custard cup upside down in center and grease will come up into glass.
- Bake potatoes quicker in a ring mold, covered.
- T.V. dinners can be heated in microwave by popping out frozen portions and heating them separately.
- To thaw 1/2 package frozen vegetables, wrap foil on portion not to be thawed. Heat, removing thawed portion.
- To shorten cooking time for soups, precook vegetables in microwave.
- Do not salt meats and vegetables on the surface before cooking.
- When baking cakes, fill only half full; place a juice glass in center of baking dish to prevent soggy middle; place cake dish on another dish or rack for bottom of cake to bake quicker. Square cakes need foil on corners; remove during final baking.
- For raising bread dough: Put dough in proper container, cover with plastic wrap and damp cloth. Heat on lowest power for 2 to 3 minutes. May repeat. Leave bread in microwave to rise.

MICROWAVE, MISCELLANEOUS

MICROWAVE FUDGE

1 (12 oz.) pkg. chocolate chips
1 tsp. vanilla

1 (14 oz.) can Eagle Brand
condensed milk

Combine chocolate chips and milk in a glass dish and microwave on HIGH for 3 minutes. Stir until melted and smooth. Mix in the vanilla. (Optional: Add 1 cup chopped black walnuts or pecans.)

Spread evenly into a foil-lined 8 inch square pan and chill until firm. Cut into squares. Serves 12.

MICROWAVE CHUNKY APPLESAUCE

3 c. peeled and chopped apples
¼ c. sugar

Cinnamon

Spread apples in a 2 quart dish and microwave 2 minutes, covered. Stir twice. Add sugar and cover, then microwave for 2 more minutes on HIGH. Sprinkle with cinnamon. Serve hot. Serves 6.

CREAM PUFFS

1 c. flour
4 eggs

½ c. butter or margarine

Place shortening and 1 cup water in a saucepan; mix well. Bring to a boil. Stir in flour and cook, stirring constantly for 1 minute or until mixture forms a ball. Remove from heat and cool. Add eggs, one at a time, beating until smooth after each addition. Drop by tablespoonfuls onto ungreased baking sheet and bake at 400°F. for about 45 minutes. Cool.

Fill with desired filling: Pudding, sweetened berries, ice cream, custard, etc.

EASY DESSERT TOPPING

1 c. confectioners sugar
Thin lemon slices

2 Tbsp. frozen lemonade
concentrate

Beat sugar and lemonade concentrate until smooth.

Serve over bread pudding, pound cake or ice cream. Garnish each serving with a thin lemon slice (or a mint leaf).

FROZEN STRAWBERRY JAM

4 c. mashed strawberries   8 c. sugar
2 pkg. Sure-Jell

Mix sugar and berries. Let stand 20 minutes. Stir 3 to 4 times.

Mix Sure-Jell into 2 cups water. Bring to boil for 1 minute. Remove from stove. Stir in berry-sugar mixture. Stir 5 minutes. Pour into sterilized glass jars. Let stand 2 days at room temperature. Tighten lids and freeze. (Spread on toast or can be poured over ice cream.)

CHOCOLATE LEAVES

2 sq. semi-sweet chocolate (or ½   1 tsp. butter
  c. chocolate chips)   Leaves

Wash and dry 2 dozen leaves of varying sizes. (Be sure they are non-poisonous leaves.)

Melt 2 squares chocolate and 1 teaspoon butter. Mix well.

Using a clean "watercolor-type" paint brush, paint chocolate on backs of leaves ⅛ inch thick, covering well. Chill until chocolate is firm. Peel chocolate leaves off of the leaves.

Decorate cakes or tarts with the chocolate leaves, or eat as candy.

INDEX OF RECIPES

45

Alphabet Hints

A is for aluminum foil. A piece of it with a knob of washing soda in a jar of water makes a silver dip cleaner.

B is for ball point ink which you can remove from vinyl by rubbing it with a slice of raw potato.

C is for camphorated oil. Applied with a soft cloth it will take white marks off furniture.

D is for drip dry. Shirts dry faster and smoother over a plastic bag put over the hanger.

E is for egg slicer. Use it for slicing mushrooms and beets as well as eggs.

F is for foam rubber. Rub it over upholstery to pick up dog and cat hairs.

G is for glycerine. Oil the mincer with it. It won't flavor the food.

H is for herbs. Keep them on the shelf in alphabetical order, so they're easy to find.

I is for icing. Add a pinch of baking soda to icing to keep moist and prevent cracking.

J is for jam. It takes less time to make if the sugar is warmed through in the oven.

K is for kneeling pad. Make it from an old hot water bottle stuffed with old nylons.

L is for lemon. A half dipped in salt cleans copper.

M is for magnet. Keep one in the sewing box to pick up pins and needles.

N is for newspapers. They make excellent window polishers.

O is for onion. Pierce it lengthwise with a skewer and it won't come to pieces when boiled.

P is for parsley. Seed watered with boiling water grows quicker.

Q is for quilt. Keep it from slipping by sewing matching material to one end and tucking it under the mattress.

R is for rubber gloves. When the right ones wear out, hang on to the left ones. Turn one inside out and you will have a pair again.

S is for soap. Rubbed on the bottom edges of a drawer it'll make it run smoothly.

T is for tea leaves. Put them around lily of the valley for more flowers.

U is for undies. Put the fragile ones in a pillowcase, tied around the top, and wash them with the rest of the washing in your machine.

V is for vinegar. Wiped over furniture before polishing gives an extra shine.

W is for window box. Put a layer of gravel over the earth, so the dirt doesn't spatter the windows.

X is for Xmas cake. The icing won't be ruined if the cake is put on the lid of the cake tin and the base over it.

Y is for yeast. It shouldn't be kept in the fridge or in a cold place, or it will die.

Z is for zipper. If it sticks, try running the lead of a pencil up and down the metal parts. It should then run smoothly.

Sandwich Fillings

Chicken and Sandwich Spread:
Add enough sandwich spread to finely chopped chicken to moisten.

Chicken and Nut:
Moisten chicken with mayonnaise. Add chopped nutmeats, lemon juice, and celery salt.

Chicken and Egg:
Combine 1 cup minced, cooked chicken, 2 hard-cooked egg yolks, 1 teaspoon chicken stock, 1 teaspoon lemon juice, and 1 teaspoon butter. Mix and spread.

Egg and Ham Salad:
Combine 6 hard-cooked eggs, diced; 1 cup cooked, diced ham; 6 sweet pickles, chopped; 1 cup chopped celery; 10 stuffed olives; and mayonnaise to moisten.

Date and Nut:
Combine 2/3 cup ground dates, 1/3 cup ground pecan meats, 1 1/2 tablespoons mayonnaise, and 1 tablespoon lemon juice. Mix and spread. Nice for rolled sandwiches.

Cream Cheese and Pineapple:
Combine cream cheese, crushed pineapple, and chopped nuts.

Ham Salad:
Combine 3/4 cup cooked, chopped ham; 1 tablespoon chopped onion; 1 hard-cooked egg, chopped; 1/4 cup chopped green peppers; and 1/4 cup mayonnaise.

Salmon and Nut:
Combine 1 cup flaked salmon, 3 tablespoons chopped nuts, 3 tablespoons minced celery, and 1/2 cup mayonnaise.

Tuna:
Combine tuna, chopped celery, walnuts and mayonnaise.

Tuna:
Combine tuna, crushed pineapple, chopped celery, and mayonnaise.

Chicken and Pineapple:
Combine 8-ounce can crushed pineapple, drained; 1 cup chopped, cooked chicken; 2 cups walnuts, chopped; and 1/2 cup cooked salad dressing. Spread between buttered slices of white bread. Remove crusts and cut each sandwich diagonally into quarters. Makes 4 dozen small sandwiches.

Pineapple and Cheese:
Combine 3 ounces cream cheese, 3 tablespoons mayonnaise, 1/2 cup chopped pecans, and 1/2 cup drained crushed pineapple. Mix and spread on crisp crackers or whole wheat bread.

General Food Hints

- An apple cut in half and placed in the cake box will keep cake fresh several days longer.
- To keep hard cheese fresh, cover with cloth moistened in vinegar; or grate the cheese and store in a tightly covered jar in the refrigerator.
- To keep sour cream fresh longer, store upside down in the refrigerator so that air cannot enter the container.
- Fresh tomatoes keep longer if stored in the refrigerator with stems down.
- Parsley will keep a long time in the refrigerator if, after washing it, you place it in a covered jar while still slightly damp.
- If soup is too salty, place a piece of raw potato in cooking pot to absorb the salty taste. If soup is too greasy, drop a lettuce leaf in pot. When grease has been absorbed, remove lettuce.
- Citrus fruit yields nearly twice the amount of juice if it is dropped into hot water a few minutes or rolled beneath your hand before squeezing.
- To peel a tomato easily, spear it with a kitchen fork and plunge it into boiling water 30 seconds. The skin will slide right off.
- Tomatoes cut vertically "bleed" less.
- Before measuring syrup, jelly, molasses, honey or other sticky substances, grease the measuring cup.
- To ignite alcohol, brandy, rum, etc., you must first heat it gently to allow the alcohol vapors to rise. If you boil the liquid, the alcohol will evaporate and never ignite.
- Before using the pulp of citrus fruits, grate the peel, being careful not to include the bitter-tasting inner white rind. Place in a tightly covered container and freeze until needed.
- For a ready supply of bread crumbs, save the heels from all your bread plus any stale bread. Place in a plastic bag and freeze until needed. Make crumbs by putting the frozen slices in a blender or food processor. You can also make crumbs first, then freeze for use in any recipe calling for fresh crumbs.
- Fried or baked chicken is especially delicious when it has first been marinated in the refrigerator overnight in buttermilk, sour milk, or sour cream.
- To keep honey from clinging to inside of measuring cup, first coat inside of cup with oil.
- You can get more juice from a dried-up lemon if you heat it for five minutes in boiling water before you squeeze it.
- When making cracker crumbs, put the crackers in a clear bag and use the rolling pin to crush them. This doesn't make a mess on the counter or the rolling pin and the crumbs can be easily poured from the bag into a measuring cup. Then shake the bag out and save it to be used again.

Substitutions

1 cup butter
1 cup margarine or 7/8 cup solid shortening + 1/2 tsp. salt

1 cup sour cream
7/8 cup sour milk + 3 Tbsp. butter; or 8-oz. carton plain yogurt

1 cup whole milk
1 cup reconstituted nonfat dry milk + 2 1/2 tsp. butter or margarine

1 cup whole milk
1/2 cup evaporated milk + 1/2 cup water

1 cup whole milk
1/4 cup sifted dry whole milk powder + 7/8 cup water

1 cup skim milk
4 Tbsp. nonfat dry milk + 1 cup water

1 cup light cream
1 cup undiluted evaporated milk

1 cup heavy cream (40%)
1/3 cup butter + 3/4 cup milk

1 cup coffee cream (20%)
3 Tbsp. butter + about 7/8 cup milk

1 cup sour milk or buttermilk
1 Tbsp. vinegar or lemon juice + enough sweet milk to make 1 cup.
(Let stand 5 minutes.)

1 tsp. lemon juice
1/2 tsp. vinegar

1 cup sweet milk
1 cup sour milk or buttermilk + 1/2 tsp. baking soda

1 cup molasses
1 cup honey

1 cup honey
1 1/4 cups sugar + 1/4 cup liquid

1 cup sugar
1 cup brown sugar, firmly packed, although it will result in a slightly molasses flavor

1 cup sugar
1/2 cup honey and reduce the amount of liquid by 1/2 cup

Hints for Pie

- A pie crust will be easier to make if all ingredients are cool.
- A teaspoon of vinegar added to pie dough helps make a flaky crust.
- Add a minimum amount of liquid to the pastry, or it will become tough.
- Pie crust will not be hard or tough when milk is used in place of the water.
- When making pie crust, add a little baking powder to keep the crust light and tender.
- Sprinkle the pastry board with 3/4 tablespoon of quick rolled oats before rolling a pie crust. It tastes nutty and provides extra nutrition.
- When baking a single pie crust, place gently in the pan and prick thoroughly. Check after baking 5 minutes and prick again in any puffed areas.
- For a single pie crust, use a scrap of pastry and press the crust against the sides of the pan so that no air can get under the crust.
- Pies should be baked in non-shiny pans to enhance the browning. Glass baking dishes also work well.
- To prevent soggy pie crusts, brush the bottom crust with egg white before pouring in fruit filling, or sprinkle with a light coating of flour and sugar.
- For a quick crust, coat a pie pan with butter and press in crushed corn flake crumbs. This is especially good with pumpkin pie.
- For a shiny pie crust, brush the top of the pie with a mixture of 1 egg, 1 teaspoon sugar, 1/4 teaspoon salt, and 1 teaspoon cooking oil. Bake as usual.
- One tablespoon of lemon Jello over apple pie before putting on the top crust will prevent runover and add flavor. Try raspberry Jello on cherry pie.
- When making pumpkin pie, separate the eggs, reserving the whites. When all ingredients are mixed, add the stiffly beaten whites for a fluffier pie.
- Put a layer of marshmallows in the bottom of a pumpkin pie, then add filling. You will have a nice topping as they come to the surface.
- Vanilla adds flavor to fruit pies.
- The meringue on pie will be higher if you add a pinch of cream of tartar to the beaten whites.
- Mix 1 teaspoon cornstarch for each egg white with the sugar, then add it to the whites for a nice meringue.
- If the juice from your apple pie runs over in the oven, shake some salt on it, which causes the juice to burn to a crisp so it can be removed.
- To prevent crust from becoming soggy with cream pie, sprinkle crust with powdered sugar.
- Folding the top crust over the lower crust before crimping will keep the juices in the pie.
- In making custard-type pies, bake at a high temperature for about ten minutes to prevent a soggy crust. Then finish baking at a low temperature.

Cookie Hints

- When using brown sugar in a recipe, always press the brown sugar firmly into the measuring cup.
- Grease the cookie sheet once — before you begin to bake — no need to grease for the rest of the batch of dough.
- Baked cookies freeze well and can be stored for several months. Pack as airtight as possible. When ready to use, thaw in refrigerator and warm in oven for a few minutes. They will taste fresh-baked.
- After melting chocolate over hot water or in microwave — cool, before adding to batter.
- Heavy, shiny cookie sheets are best for baking. When using lightweight sheets, reduce oven temperature slightly.
- When sprinkling sugar on cookies, put sugar in shaker first. Dry Jello may be added to sugar for variation.
- Before rolling, chill cookie dough in refrigerator for 30 to 60 minutes. Less dusting flour or powdered sugar will be needed. Too much flour rolled into cookies can cause them to be tough.
- To cream butter or margarine, allow it to reach room temperature. While this requires planning ahead, melting the shortening would make the batter too liquid.
- When baking cookies, use center shelf of oven only. Sheets on 2 levels will cause uneven distribution of heat.
- Place a piece of fresh baked bread in the cookie jar to keep the cookies soft and chewy.
- Many cookie recipes call for too much sugar. You can cut down on the sugar as much as half, particularly if you are using raisins, dates, chocolate chips, etc.
- When making filled cookies, use a melon ball cutter. Scoop out dough and you have a round ball.
- Cut bar cookies or rolled cookies with a pizza cutter.
- Use the doughnut cutter for rolled cookies for the children. Hole in the center is great for little ones to hold.
- When rolling out sugar cookies, use powdered sugar instead of flour.
- If you put marshmallows in the refrigerator the night before you use them, they won't stick to the shears.
- To powder sugar: When you run out of powdered sugar, blend 1 cup granulated sugar and 1 tablespoon cornstarch in blender at medium speed for 2 minutes.
- Add 2 eggs and 1/2 cup cooking oil to any flavor cake mix and you have a quick batch of cookies. Raisins, nuts or coconut can be added, if desired. Drop by teaspoonfuls onto slightly-greased cookie sheets. Bake at 350° for 8 to 10 minutes.
- Cookies that are too crisp may have too much sugar in the dough.
- Cookies that are too soft usually have too much liquid in proportion to the flour.

Hints for Cakes & Frostings

• Have all ingredients at room temperature.
• Fill cake pans about 2/3 full and spread batter well into corners and to the sides, leaving a slight hollow in center.
• The cake is done when it shrinks slightly from the sides of the pan or if it springs back when touched lightly with the finger.
• After a cake comes from the oven, it should be placed on a rack for about five minutes. Then the sides should be loosened and the cake turned out onto rack to finish cooling.
• Cakes should not be frosted until thoroughly cooled.
• Roll fruits and raisins in flour before adding them to the cake batter so they will stay distributed throughout the cake.
• When adding dry and wet ingredients, such as flour and milk, begin and end with the dry ingredients, beating well after each addition for a smoother batter.
• If eggs are not beaten well or ingredients not thoroughly mixed, a coarse-grained cake will result.
• For an interesting flavor, add a melted chocolate mint to chocolate cake batter.
• To keep chocolate cakes brown on the outside, dust the greased pan with cocoa instead of flour.
• If baking in glass dishes, decrease the oven temperature 25° to prevent overbrowning.
• Use the circular cardboards from the bottom of frozen pizzas when transporting a cake. Cover with foil first.
• If a layer cake comes out lopsided, insert marshmallows between the bottom layer and the cake plate, or wherever they are needed.
• Stir 3 ounces of chocolate chips into 7-minute frosting while it is still hot to make it creamy and delicious.
• When frosting a cake, place strips of waxed paper beneath the edges of the cake. They can easily be removed after frosting.
• For a different frosting, mix 2 tablespoons of pineapple and 2 tablespoons of orange juice. Add enough powdered sugar to stiffen.
• Sprinkle applesauce cake or banana cake generously with granulated sugar, coconut and chopped nuts before baking. It makes a crunchy topping.
• When melting chocolate, grease pan in which it is to be melted.
• When you are creaming butter and sugar together, it's a good idea to rinse the bowl with boiling water first. They'll cream faster.
• When you buy cellophane-wrapped cupcakes and notice that the cellophane is somewhat stuck to the frosting, hold the package under the cold water tap for a moment before you unwrap it. The cellophane will then come off clean.
• A clean clothespin provides a cool handle to steady the cake tin when removing a hot cake.
• Try using a thread instead of a knife when a cake is to be cut while it is hot.

BAKING TIPS

CAUSES OF PROBLEMS

BISCUITS
Rough biscuits   Insufficient mixing.
Dry biscuits   Baking in too slow an oven and handling
                                  too much.
Uneven browning   Cooking in dark surface pan, too high a
                                  temperature and rolling the dough too thin.

BREADS (yeast)
Porous bread   Over-rising or cooking at too low a temper-
                                  ature.
Crust is dark and blisters   Under-rising.
  just under the crust.
Bread does not rise   Over-kneading or using old yeast.
Bread is streaked   Under-kneading and not kneading evenly.
Bread baked unevenly   Using old, dark pans; too much dough in pan;
                                  crowding the oven shelf or cooking at too
                                  high a temperature.

CAKES
Cracks; uneven surface   Too much flour; too hot an oven and some-
                                  times from cold oven start.
Dry cakes   Too much flour; too little shortening; too
                                  much baking powder; or cooking at too
                                  low a temperature.
Heavy cakes   Too much sugar or baking too short a period.
Sticky crust   Too much sugar.
Coarse grained cake   Too little mixing; too much shortening; too
                                  much baking powder; using shortening too
                                  soft; and baking at too low a temperature.
Fallen cakes   Using insufficient flour; underbaking; too
                                  much sugar; too much shortening; or not
                                  enough baking powder.
Uneven color   Cooking at too high a temperature; crowding
                                  the shelf (allow at least 2 inches around
                                  pans) or using dark pans.
Uneven browning   Not mixing well.

COOKIES
Uneven browning   Not using shiny cookie sheet or not allowing
                                  at least 2 inches on all sides of cookie
                                  sheets in oven.
Soggy cookies   Cooling cookies in pans instead of racks.
Excessive spreading   Dropping cookies onto hot cookie sheets;
  of cookies   not baking at correct temperature.

MUFFINS
Coarse texture   Insufficient stirring and cooking at too low a
                                  temperature.
Tunnels in muffins; peaks   Over-mixing.
  in center; soggy texture

PIES
Pastry crumbles   Over-mixing flour and shortening.
Pastry tough   Using too much water and over-mixing the
                                  dough.
Pies do not brown   Bake at constant temperature (400-425°) in
                                  (fruit or custard) Pyrex or enamel pie pan.

54

General Oven Chart

Very Slow Oven .... 250°-300°F.	Med. Hot Oven .... 375°-400°F.	
Slow Oven .... 300°-325°F.	Hot Oven .... 400°-450°F.	
Moderate Oven .... 325°-375°F.	Very Hot Oven .... 450°-500°F.	

Breads

Baking Powder Biscuits	450°F.	12-15 minutes
Muffins	400°-425°F.	20-25 minutes
Quick Breads	350°F.	40-60 minutes
Yeast Breads	375°-400°F.	45-60 minutes
Yeast Rolls	400°F.	15-20 minutes

Cakes

Butter Loaf Cakes	350°F.	45-60 minutes
Butter Layer Cakes	350°-375°F.	25-35 minutes
Cupcakes	375°F.	20-25 minutes
Chiffon Cakes	325°F.	60 minutes
Sponge Cakes	325°F.	60 minutes
Angel Food Cakes	325°F.	60 minutes

Cookies

Bar Cookies	350°F.	25-30 minutes
Drop Cookies	350°-375°F.	8-12 minutes
Rolled and Ref. Cookies	350°-400°F.	8-12 minutes

Pastry

Meringues	350°F.	12-20 minutes
Pie Shells	450°F.	12-15 minutes
Filled Pies	450°F.	10 minutes
	lower to 350°F.	40 minutes

Roasts

Beef Roast		
Rare	325°F.	18-20 min. per lb.
Medium	325°F.	22-25 min. per lb.
Well done	325°F.	30 min. per lb.
Chicken	325°-350°F.	30 min. per lb.
Duck	325°-350°F.	25 min. per lb.
Fish Fillets	500°F.	15-20 min. per lb.
Goose	325°-350°F.	30 min. per lb.
Ham	350°F.	20-30 min. per lb.
Lamb	300°-350°F.	35 min. per lb.
Meat Loaf	375°F.	60 min. for 2 lb. loaf
Pork Roast	350°F.	30 min. per lb.
Turkey	250°-325°F.	15-25 min. per lb.
Veal Roast	300°F.	30 min. per lb.
Venison	350°F.	20-25 min. per lb.

Planning for a Crowd

Foods	Servings	Serving Unit	Amt. to Purchase
BEVERAGES			
Coffee, ground	40-50	3/4 c.	1 lb. (5 c.)
Cream for coffee	25	1 Tbsp.	1 pt.
Milk	24	1 c.	1 1/2 gal.
Tea, leaves	50	3/4 c.	1 c.
DESSERTS			
Cake	24	2 1/2" squares	(1) 15 1/2 x 10 1/2 x 1-in sheet cake
Ice cream	24	1/2 c. or 1 slice	3 qts.
Pie	30	1/6 of pie	(5) 9-in. pies
Whipped cream	25	2 Tbsps.	1 pt.
FRUIT			
Canned	24	1/2 c.	(1) 6 1/2- or 7 1/4-lb. can
MEAT			
Beef roast, chuck	25	4 ozs.	12 1/4 lbs., bone in
Ground beef	25	3-oz. pattie	6 3/4 lbs.
Ham, baked, sliced	25	4 ozs.	10 lbs., boneless
Chicken	24	1/4 chicken	6 chickens
Turkey -	25	3 ozs.	15 lbs.
Turkey, roll, precooked	25	3 ozs.	6-7 lbs.
PASTA, RICE			
Rice, long-grain	24	1/2 c., cooked	1 1/2 lbs., uncooked
Spaghetti and noodles	25	3/4 c., cooked	2 1/2 lbs., uncooked
RELISHES			
(combine several)			
Carrot strips	25	2-3 strips	1 lb.
Celery	25	(1) 2-3" piece	1 lb.
Olives	25	3-4 olives	1 qt.
Pickles	25	1 oz.	1 qt.
SALADS			
Fruit	24	1/3 c.	2 qts.
Potato	24	1/2 c.	3 qts.
Tossed vegetable	25	3/4 c.	5 qts.
Salad dressing	32	1 Tbsp.	1 pt.
SOUP	25	1 c. (main course)	1 1/2 gals. or (2) 50-oz. cans, condensed
VEGETABLES			
Canned	25	1/2 c.	(1) 6 1/2 - to 7 1/4-lb can
Fresh:			
Lettuce, for salad (Iceberg)	24	1/6 head, raw	4 heads
Potatoes, mashed	25	1/2 c., mashed	6 3/4 lbs., raw
Potatoes, baked	25	1 medium	8 1/2 lbs., raw
Frozen:			
Beans, green or wax	25	1/3 c.	5 1/4 lbs.
Carrots	25	1/3 c., sliced	5 lbs.
Corn, whole kernel	25	1/3 c.	5 lbs.
Peas	25	1/3 c.	5 lbs.
Potatoes, French fried	25	10 pieces	3 1/4 lbs.
MISCELLANEOUS			
Butter 32	1 pat	1/2 lb.	
Juice	23	1/2 c.	(2) 46-oz. cans
Potato chips	25	3/4 - 1 oz.	1 - 1 1/2 lbs.
French bread	24	3/4-in. slice	(1) 18-in. loaf

Food Quantities for 25, 50 and 100 Servings

FOOD	25 Servings	50 Servings	100 Servings
Soup & Sandwiches:			
Rolls	4 doz.	8 doz.	16 doz.
Bread	50 slices	100 slices	200 slices
	(3) 1-lb. loaves	(6) 1-lb. loaves	(12) 1-lb. loaves
Butter	1/2 lb.	3/4 - 1 lb.	1 1/2 lbs.
Mayonnaise	1 c.	2 - 3 c.	4 - 6 c.
Mixed filling for sandwiches			
(meat, eggs, fish)	1 1/2 qts.	2 1/2 - 3 qts.	5 - 6 qts.
Mixed filling (sweet-fruit)	1 qt.	1 3/4 - 2 qts.	2 1/2 - 4 qts.
Jams & preserves	1 1/2 lbs.	3 lbs.	6 lbs.
Crackers	1 1/2 lbs.	3 lbs.	6 lbs.
Cheese (2 oz.)	3 lbs.	6 lbs.	12 lbs.
Soup	1 1/4 gal.	2 1/2 gal.	5 gal.
Salad dressings	1 pt.	2 1/2 pts.	1/2 gal.
Meat, Poultry or Fish:			
Wieners (beef)	6 1/2 lbs.	13 lbs.	25 lbs.
Hamburger	9 lbs.	18 lbs.	35 lbs.
Turkey or chicken	13 lbs.	25 - 35 lbs.	50 - 75 lbs.
Fish, large whole (round)	13 lbs.	25 lbs.	50 lbs.
Fish, fillets or steaks	7 1/2 lbs.	15 lbs.	30 lbs.
Meat Loaf	6 lbs.	12 lbs.	24 lbs.
Ham	10 lbs.	20 lbs.	40 lbs.
Salads, Casseroles, Vegetables:			
Potato salad	4 1/4 qts.	2 1/4 gal.	4 1/2 gal.
Scalloped potatoes	4 1/2 qts. or	8 1/2 qts.	17 qts.
	(1) 12x20" pan		
Mashed potatoes	9 lbs.	18 - 20 lbs.	25 - 35 lbs.
Spaghetti	1 1/4 gal.	2 1/2 gal.	5 gal.
Baked beans	3/4 gal.	1 1/4 gal.	2 1/2 gal.
Jello salad	3/4 gal.	1 1/4 gal.	2 1/2 gal.
Canned vegetables	(1)#10 can	(2 1/2) #10 cans	(4)#10 cans
Lettuce (for salads)	4 heads	8 heads	15 heads
Cabbage (for slaw)	5 lbs.	10 lbs.	20 lbs.
Carrots (3 oz. or 1/2 c.)	6 1/4 lbs.	12 1/2 lbs.	25 lbs.
Tomatoes	3 - 5 lbs.	7 - 10 lbs.	14 - 20 lbs.
Desserts:			
Watermelon	37 1/2 lbs.	75 lbs.	150 lbs.
Fruit cup (1/2 c.)	3 qts.	6 qts.	12 qts.
Cake	(1) 10x12"	(1) 12x20"	(2) 12x20"
	sheet cake	sheet cake	sheet cakes
	(1 1/2) 10"	(3) 10"	(6) 10"
	layer cakes	layer cakes	layer cakes
Whipping cream	3/4 pt.	1 1/2 - 2 pts.	3 pts.
Ice Cream:			
Brick	3 1/4 qts.	6 1/2 qts.	12 1/2 qts.
Bulk	2 1/4 qts.	4 1/2 qts. or	9 qts. or
		1 1/4 gal.	2 1/2 gal.
Beverages:			
Coffee	1/2 lb. and	1 lb. and	2 lbs. and
	1 1/2 gal. water	3 gal. water	6 gal. water
Tea	1/12 lb. and	1/6 lb. and	1/3 lb. and
	1 1/2 gal. water	3 gal. water	6 gal. water
Lemonade	10 - 15 lemons	20 - 30 lemons	40 - 60 lemons
	1 1/2 gal. water	3 gal. water	6 gal. water

Miscellaneous Helpful Hints

- Stained hands from vegetables during canning season can be cured by rubbing your hands with a sliced potato.
- After dressing chickens, fish or cutting onions, pour vinegar or lemon juice into the palm of one hand and rub your hands together. Wash with soap.
- Put 1 Tbsp. soda and salt in scalding water when dressing chickens. Pin feathers will come out easily, or add one cup of vinegar to 8-10 quarts of water.
- If a cracked dish is boiled for 45 minutes in sweet milk, the crack will be so welded together that it will hardly be visible, and will be so strong it will stand the same usage as before.
- Occasionally throw a little salt on burning logs to keep the chimney clean.
- You can make your own liquid soap by shaving bar soap into a dish, then covering it with water and putting it in the microwave oven. In less than a minute the soap dissolves into a liquid.
- To remove a broken light bulb from a socket, insert a large cork into the socket and turn it out.
- Did you know that you can stop a door hinge from creaking by rubbing it with a lead pencil?
- Spray garbage sacks with ammonia to prevent dogs from tearing the bags before picked up.
- Glycerin makes an excellent lubricant for egg beaters or other kitchen utensils that have moving parts. Unlike oil, it will not spoil the taste of food mixed with it by accident. The glycerin may be applied with a medicine dropper.
- A cheap brand of lawn fertilizer will melt snow and ice just as quickly as salt. It will benefit your lawn instead of killing it.
- Pop your contact paper in the freezer about an hour before you use it and it will handle much easier.
- When the tip of a shoestring comes off, dip the end of the lace in clear fingernail polish and let dry. You will have a hard-tipped shoestring again for easier lacing.
- Put your old rubber bathtub or sink mats in the car trunk or truck. They give good traction on ice when slipped under the tires. Pour some household bleach over your tires, wait 10 minutes and drive off carefully.
- If you have one of those instant - on T.V. sets, unplug it when not in use. These sets use and waste electricity even when they're turned off.
- Unwrap bar soap before storing. It will harden and last longer besides giving your cupboard a pleasant fragrance.
- Pam (vegetable spray-on product for cooking) sprayed along the metal frames of windows will keep them moving without a battle. Repeat as needed.
- Nylon net makes a good vegetable brush or is good for cleaning fish aquariums, filter tubes or any hard-to-clean glass surface. Use it for washing plucked and singed chickens, too.
- When hanging pictures, heat the nail with a flame before driving it into the wall. You won't crack or chip the plaster.

• If your fireplace needs kindling, save waxed cardboard milk and ice cream cartons. These all kindle quickly.

• Organize a toy lending library or swap toys with other mothers in the neighborhood.

• Damp leather shoes can be reconditioned in the following manner: Dry them thoroughly, clean them with saddle soap, and rub them gently with castor oil.

• If you are painting with an oil-base paint and need to stop for a short time, wrap the brush in aluminum foil and place in the freezer until ready to return to the job. The paint will not harden.

• A quick way to shovel the front steps after a snowfall is with a dustpan. It is quick, easy and efficient. Work from the bottom step up.

• Moving to an apartment or smaller home and need to reduce storage items? Send old photos that you no longer need to those who are in the picture. You have no idea how pleased one will be to get a long forgotten picture.

• A light coating of frost or ice can be removed from your windshield by spraying it with windshield washer solution.

• A generous amount of plain table salt applied to the top of a tree stump will kill the tree when the sap goes down to the roots in the fall.

• To keep hornets from nesting under LP valve covers, paint the area with ordinary gun grease. They don't like grease on their wings.

• That plastic clothes basket can also be used to get everything to the pool or beach. Not only does it reduce the number of items to be carried, but it can hold the wet suits and towels on the return directly to the laundry room!

• A bathtub toy that provides great fun is an empty thread spool. Dampen it and rub one end on a soft bar of soap. Blow through the hole and see all the bubbles it makes.

• To help explain age to your pre-schooler, take a measuring tape and say each inch stands for one year of a person's age. Children can then "see" how old other persons are compared to them.

ICE BUCKET

• Use your insulated ice bucket all summer. Fill it with ice cubes in the morning and place on the kitchen counter. When the family wants a cold drink, they won't have to open the freezer to get their ice cubes.

• No need to use the insulated ice bucket just for ice. It can be a handy carrier for either hot or cold foods. Carry it to your next picnic or potluck supper and foods will retain their temperature and taste better.

BUDGET

• Put a time limit on your major weekly shopping trip to the supermarket since this will likely save you money. Shopping for a longer time than 30 minutes usually means you wind up buying unnecessary items. The average amount spent grocery shopping is about 95¢ per minute.

• Pay your insurance policies on an annual basis and total your savings. You will be pleased.

CAR
• Except for housing and food, nothing consumes a bigger slice of your budget than your car. Keep your car in good shape with regular tune-ups. Keep a record on your car's good health.

• Check to see whether any of the spark plugs are misfiring. One plug that misses on an 8-cylinder engine can hike gas consumption by as much as 12%. On a 4-cylinder engine, the figure rises to 25%.

• Avoid prolonged car idling. Idling the engine for more than a minute uses more fuel than is required to restart your engine after shutting it off.

• Keep the car tires properly inflated. Underinflated tires can reduce gas mileage by as much as 10%.

FURNITURE
• If summer outdoor furniture doesn't respond to ordinary cleaning, try adding chlorine bleach to the cleaning water for plastic furniture.

• Aluminum lawn furniture may be pitted and this wear can sometimes be smoothed with soap-filled steel wool pads.

• Plastic lids can be saved to place under the legs of furniture after shampooing and cleaning rugs. Leave until the rugs dry and there will be no danger of rust spots.

SMALL APPLIANCES
• Slow cookers should be at least half full for best results.

• Use small appliances such as slow cookers or electric fry pans for cooking. They generally use less energy than a gas or electric range for cooking the same foods.

• To convert recipes for use in your slow cooker or crock pot, usually 1 hour of conventional cooking at 350° equals 8 hours of slow cooking on low setting or 4 hours on the high setting.

• If fried foods are forbidden and you wonder what to do with your French fryer, use it for boiling potatoes. When the potatoes are done, just lift the basket out of the pan and drain.

• Another idea for the French fryer basket is to use it for cooking macaroni, noodles, or spaghetti. Lift the basket from the water and the contents will be ready to be rinsed and transferred to another bowl.

Hints for Gifts

• For the person on your list who has everything, give a gift of food. Your special coffeecake or salad dressing with the recipe included will be most welcome.

• Give food gifts in a special container. Bread may be given in a bread basket or loaf tin, beverages in decanters or pitchers, nuts or candy in a lovely jar or brandy snifter. At Christmas, fasten a bow with a sprig of evergreen.

• Practical gifts for children bring more pleasure if there's a surprise tucked inside. For instance, a pair of pajamas could have bedtime stories tucked in and each finger of a pair of gloves might hold a small coin.

• Enclose the label showing washing or cleaning instructions for the yarn when giving a homemade crocheted or knitted article.

• Give a gift that will encourage the recipient to expand, to open a new door that will bring their creativity and innate ability out into the open.

• Bird feeders or bird houses make a fine gift for the bird watcher.

• Magazine subscriptions will be appreciated year 'round. Give either a magazine the person reads regularly or a new one to develop additional reading sampling.

• What new bride wouldn't treasure a notebook of recipes from relatives and friends. This takes time so start months before the wedding.

• Ask each guest at a bridal shower to give her favorite household hint to you. Roll these inside an empty pill bottle and call it a prescription of hints and advice.

• A tape recorder is a thoughtful gift for grandparents who live far away. Get one for yourself too, and you can exchange verbal messages for years to come.

• Like to give money for a gift but have no new bills? Take a bill that is in fairly good condition (not damaged or worn) and wash it with warm water and mild soapsuds. Place between the folds of a cloth and press with a warm iron. It will look like new!

• Children with more time than money can give gift coupons to parents or grandparents. "Good for one Sunday breakfast in bed" or "Good for one car wash."

• A gourmet cook would appreciate fresh herbs such as chives or basil growing in pretty pots to place on the window sill.

• If you have trouble cutting gift wrapping paper with a straight edge, keep your eyes on the point of the scissors. It is intriguing and never fails.

Traditional Wedding Anniversary Gift List

First: Paper
Second: Cotton
Third: Leather
Fourth: Fruit and Flowers
Fifth: Wood
Sixth: Sugar and Candy
Seventh: Wool
Eighth: Pottery
Ninth: Willow
Tenth: Tin
Eleventh: Steel
Twelfth: Silk and Linen

Thirteenth: Lace
Fourteenth: Ivory
Fifteenth: Crystal
Twentieth: China
Twenty-Fifth: Silver
Thirtieth: Pearl
Thirty-Fifth: Coral
Fortieth: Ruby
Forty-Fifth: Sapphire
Fiftieth: Gold
Seventy-Fifth: Diamond

Modern Wedding Anniversary Gift List

1st	Clock	14th	Gold Jewelry
2nd	China	15th	Watches
3rd	Crystal, glass	16th	Silver Hollow ware
4th	Electrical appliances	17th	Furniture
5th	Silverware	18th	Porcelain
6th	Wood	19th	Bronze
7th	Desk Sets, Pen and Pencil Sets	20th	Platinum
8th	Linens, Laces	25th	Sterling Silver Jubilee
9th	Leather	30th	Diamond
10th	Diamond Jewelry	35th	Jade
11th	Fashion Jewelry and Accessories	40th	Ruby
		45th	Sapphire
12th	Pearls or Colored Gems	50th	Golden Jubilee
		55th	Emerald
13th	Textiles, Furs	60th	Diamond Jubilee

Month	Birthstone	Flower
January	Garnet	Carnation
February	Amethyst	Primrose
March	Bloodstone	Violet
April	Diamond	Daisy
May	Emerald	Peony
June	Agate and Pearl	Rose
July	Ruby	Water Lilly
August	Sardonyx	Poppy
September	Sapphire	Aster
October	Opal	Calendula
November	Topaz	Chrysanthemum
December	Turquoise	Poinsettia

For All Your Printing Needs........

Blue & Grey Book Shoppe
& Press

107 W. Lexington
Independence, Missouri 64050
816-252-9909
http://blueandgrey.com

Single Copy to Manuscript

Full service print shop offering:
-Printing
-Binding
-Collating

Short Runs Welcome!

Ruthie Wornall has been collecting easy recipes for nearly twenty years. She admits she was not a good cook when she was first married, but says these easy recipes helped it appear that she was. Her recipes are so fast and easy that she often prepares an entire dinner on television in ten minutes..

Ruthie, a former school teacher in Raytown, Missouri, is married to Jim Wornall, a second vice president at a corporation in Overland Park, Kansas, and they have two children who are still in school.

Ruthie writes the "Reluctant Chef" food column for the Weston Chronicle Newspaper in Weston, Missouri as well as the "Recipe Corner" food column for the Newton County Times Newspaper in Jasper, Arkansas. She is active in a Baptist church, and volunteers weekly at a nursing home where her children occasionally sing and play piano for the residents.

Ruthie has written a series of 11 cookbooks. They are: the Three Ingredient Cookbook, Volumes I, II, and III; the Low-Cholesterol Three Ingredient Cookbook; the Three Ingredient Party Cookbook; the Three Ingredient Main Dish Cookbook; the Two Ingredient Cookbook; the Low-Fat Three Ingredient Cookbook, and the Low-Sugar Three Ingredient Cookbook.

The most recent books have hardback covers and are: The Best of the 3 Ingredient Cookbook and the Three Ingredient Low-Fat Cookbook which are now available.

ISBN 0-962446

$6.95

0695

9 780962 446702